Douglas Earle Marsh

His Life and Times

by
Klaus Marx

THE OAKWOOD PRESS

British Library Cataloguing in Publication Data
A Record for this book is available from the British Library
ISBN 0 85361 633 7

Typeset by Oakwood Graphics.
Repro by Ford Graphics, Ringwood, Hants.
Printed by Cambrian Printers, Aberystwyth, Dyfed.

Marsh Atlantic No. 41 exits Victoria with the non-stop Pullman express to Brighton. This train originated as the 'Pullman Limited' of 1881, renamed the 'Brighton Limited' in 1899 and the 'Southern Belle' in 1908. This duty was given to the new 'Hs'. The photograph presents a stirring image of the bustling smoke-saturated approach to the Brighton's West London terminus which was rebuilt in stages from 1905 and formally reopened on 1st July. 1908. *R.C. Riley Collection*

Front cover: LB&SCR class 'H2' 4-4-2 No. 422 with the 'Southern Belle' leaving Victoria *c.*1914
Rear cover, top: Atlantic express locomotive of the London Brighton & South Coast Railway.
Rear cover, bottom: LB&SCR No. 326 4-6-2 tank locomotive.

Title page: Bessborough was painted out in umber livery before entering general service in March 1912. It is seen here with the 'Southern Belle' Pullmans standing outside Brighton, possibly on a test run. *R.C. Riley Collection*

Published by The Oakwood Press (Usk), P.O. Box 13, Usk, Mon., NP15 1YS.
E-mail: sales@oakwoodpress.co.uk
Website: www.oakwood-press.co.uk

Contents

A superb study of the LB&SCR's flagship of the time, the pioneer Marsh Atlantic 'H1' class No. 37, standing on the west side turntable outside Victoria between Elizabeth and Ebury Street bridges. The locomotive's pristine condition suggests an official photograph taken at the time it entered traffic on the Brighton-Victoria expresses in the spring of 1906. This splendid portrait brings out the beautiful lines of the Marsh-liveried design.

Fred Stone Memorial Collection/Bluebell Archives

Introduction

This has been a difficult biography to write. The professional historian must always attempt to establish and arrive at the truth and yet seek to cover the subject sympathetically. 'Warts and all' it may be, but the kernel of truth in this case has been overlaid by layer upon layer of rumour and fabrication, blown out of all proportion to the facts.

Douglas Earle Marsh and his family suffered more hurt and humiliation than was merited and, after such high career expectations, Marsh's prospects were shattered and the rest of his life a 'come down'. Ill health as a result of the stresses and trauma of his period at Brighton certainly played a part in all of this.

I make no apologies for the lengthy chapter featuring Marsh's relationship with the railway's workforce, since in this section we have the only real insight into the man himself. His very words taken down verbatim give us an insight into his character and temperament that help in part to explain the astonishing saga of his life. In this folder of documents, which survive in the National Archives, Kew, we can follow every twist and turn in the wrestling match between the embattled locomotive superintendent and his unsympathetic operatives, though the episodes selected comprise but a fraction of the whole.

The material for this book has come from many quarters. I should like to acknowledge the contributions of Philip Evetts, whose recollections are based on talks with Jack Marsh who was a pupil apprentice at the Great Western Railway (GWR) Works at Swindon when he started there in 1931, together with elderly colleagues who knew Marsh senior at Swindon; former employees of the London, Brighton & South Coast Railway (LB&SCR) and such Brighton authorities as Brailsford and Maskelyne; Peter Treloar for allowing me to peruse the material in the collection Jack Marsh bequeathed to the Firefly Trust at Didcot Railway Centre. I should also like to thank my fellow members of the Brighton Circle, especially Jonathan Abson, Gerard Collins, Mike Cruttenden, Edward Hart, Charles Long, John Minnis, Fred Rich, Dick Riley and Nick Wellings for their help and advice, Lawrence Marshall who has supplied the bulk of the photographs from his comprehensive LB&SCR collection (where there is no acknowledgement to a photograph, it comes from Lawrence's collection), and especially to the late John Hull for typing out my copy to disc.

I have to stand alongside Phil Evetts in apologising for airing the variously disparaging balloons of calumny, but trust to have shot down many kites without foundation, leaving the sifted evidence of what was heard at first hand or has already been in print. It stands as a sorry story of human lack of charity. Whatever happened in Marsh's personal life, the brilliance of the 'I3' tanks and his 'Brighton Atlantics' remains an outstanding achievement of his day that will not walk away.

Chapter One

Induction

Early Years

Despite many previous mentions that Douglas Earle Marsh was born at Brighton, it is now widely accepted that he first saw the light of day in the village of Salle in North Norfolk, the second son of the Rector, Charles Earle Marsh and his wife (née Catherine Steed), on the 4th January, 1862. A memorial plaque was later placed in the parish church there.

Nothing is known of his childhood until the age of 16 when he followed his elder brother, Herbert, to the public school at Brighton College, remaining there for two years. It is possible that whilst at Brighton he became drawn to the world of the railway shops there under the impressive regime of William Stroudley and his attractive locomotives, and set his heart on a career in railway engineering.

From there he went to University College, London, in 1879 to study under Professor Kennedy Pure and Applied Mathematics, Physics, Mechanical Drawing, Geology, Mineralogy, Engineering and Mechanical Technology, Surveying and Engineering Drawing, obtaining a range of 2nd and 3rd class certificates during the three-year course. He lodged at 23 Bristol Gardens, Paddington, the home of Charles Schneider, Professor of Languages, his wife and four young daughters.

His respectable, if undistinguished, progress was sufficient to be taken on, in October 1881, as an apprenticed pupil of William Dean, locomotive superintendent of the Great Western Railway at Swindon. He was subsequently employed as a draughtsman and later as an inspector of materials. When the vacancy for an assistant works manager occurred in May 1889, he was offered the post and he accepted. His early promotion became quickly soured when an unfortunate conflict of personalities occurred resulting in Marsh and his works manager, H. Carlton, not being on speaking terms. The latter's dislike for Marsh became so intense that he shunned all personal contact and refused to delegate responsibility for even routine matters.

Marsh endured this agonising situation for six years, but near the end of his time at Swindon in 1895 the Doublebois derailment occurred when two 0-4-4 tanks, working in tandem, came off the rails at high speed while working a Plymouth-Penzance express. This occurrence, incidentally, created in him an intense dislike of front-coupled tank engines. The class was notoriously unsteady. H. Holcroft, an apprentice at Wolverhampton, took out one of the class on a trial trip following repairs, the driver on the return trip being instructed to run as fast as possible. He wrote afterwards, 'There was never a trip like this. It had to be experienced to be believed, for the lateral oscillation was terrific; the motion implanted to those on the footplate could be likened to terrier shaking a rat'.

At the end of the album described in the adjacent paragraph, Marsh in his own writing has compiled a list of dimensions of locomotives that particularly interested him.

The Firefly Trust

Swindon works memo sheet found in the Marsh memorabilia. *Firefly Trust*

The Earle Marsh Collection

By good fortune, some of the memorabilia of Marsh's early period at Swindon have survived to reside in the Firefly Trust of which his son, Jack, was a founder member and director. The Trust was incorporated in 1982 with the aim of constructing a replica of Daniel Gooch's 'Firefly' class of locomotive, the Great Western Railway's first standard broad-gauge design of 1840. In 1985, Jack Marsh presented the collection of his father's photographs, drawings etc. to the Trust.

Prominent is an album of superb locomotive photographs, which Peter Treloar has edited under the title *The Earle Marsh Album*. What governed Marsh's selection is unclear, though the batch of Great Eastern Railway portraits could derive from his friendship with James Holden, who was a colleague at Swindon before moving to Stratford. The album, which includes fine sharp prints of 54 GWR locomotives and 21 shared among nine other railway companies (but not the LB&SCR) appears to have been compiled by Marsh, at the end of which he included a tabular list of dimensions for each. The latest locomotive depicted in the original album dates from 1887, though there are a further number of loose photographs dating from 1888 through to 1891, but these are not registered in the aforesaid table, indicating that Marsh most likely put the album together in the year preceding his appointment as assistant works manager.

It was in this capacity that Marsh supervised the draughtsmen's designs and another large book, entitled *Locomotive Details*, included the arrangement of underframes, spring gear on tenders, oil axle boxes, several frame plans, arrangements of horn blocks, foundation rings, and chimney blast pipe,

Marsh's written instructions to one of his draughtsmen at Swindon. *The Firefly Trust*

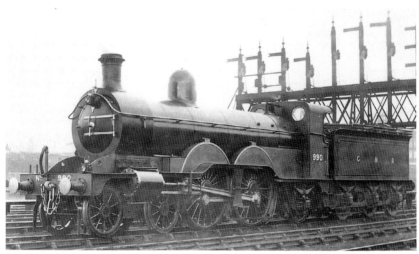

No. 990 the prototype Atlantic completed at Doncaster in May 1898, with the construction of which Marsh, as chief assistant mechanical engineer and works manager, was closely involved. It was some time before the name *Henry Oakley* was applied. The new 4-4-2 is seen here at a location believed to be York by virtue of the North Eastern Railway vehicles in the background. The class were called 'Klondykes' after the contemporary gold-rush.

together with alterations to the leading end of narrow-gauge engines. On a loose sheet (*illustrated*) Marsh, obviously not fully satisfied with the draughtsman's results, requested particulars, stating, 'This measurement is not known in either of the above drawings referred to'. Most of the drawings date from December 1895, a few weeks before Marsh moved on to Doncaster.

Two other batches of photographs remain to be described, namely a number of enlarged ones of various locomotives on large boards which includes one of Great Northern Railway small Atlantic No. 990, ex-works and prior to it receiving the name *Henry Oakley*. This was doubtless treasured by Marsh as he would have worked closely on the later stages of construction of Henry Ivatt's revolutionary creation, the first 4-4-2 to be built in this country, which was completed at Doncaster in May 1898. The first impression made on Marsh was to remain the seed idea he later developed at Brighton.

The other group includes the construction of bridges, showing the Forth Bridge being built and another across a river estuary in South Wales. It is not possible to be sure that the youthful figure portrayed in one of these, is of young Marsh himself, though it was common practice to give young locomotive apprentices experience in other engineering departments. Together with these are several fine photographs of national features not too far from Swindon, for instance, Salisbury Cathedral and Market Cross, Stonehenge, Chepstow Castle and Bridge and Tintern Abbey, all in late Victorian days, together with a family group. It has been suggested that these portraits could well have been sourced from the GWR's official photographs that were reproduced in carriage compartments.

Doncaster

The previously described untoward events may well have spurred Marsh to apply for a post elsewhere and at the end of 1895 he had the good fortune to be appointed chief assistant mechanical engineer and manager of the Great Northern Railway's Doncaster works under Henry A. Ivatt who succeeded as CME following the death of Robert Patrick Stirling who had been in charge there since 1866. Both new men, who took up their appointments at the start of 1896, fully appreciated the need for co-operation and came to trust each other so much so that, on one occasion when obliged to take an extended vacation for reasons of health, Ivatt was content to leave the responsibility of supervising the works entirely to his assistant. Marsh was elected M.I.Mech.E that same year. According to Anthony Bulleid, Marsh proved an admirable works manager and chief assistant, and made major contributions to the design and layout of the Crimpsall area of Doncaster works.

The new team soon improved the efficiency of the works, increasing the annual production of new locomotives by a third and introduced more advanced and purposeful designs. Marsh appeared to enjoy good relations with his colleagues, and was part of the team that produced a series of small 4-4-2 tanks in 1898 and saw the introduction of the small Atlantics and, four years later No. 251, the first of the large Atlantics with a wide-based firebox, designs that influenced greatly his future thinking. According to Charles Fryer, it is very likely indeed that it was Marsh who suggested the wider firebox design in the first place.

Marsh at this period had opportunity to travel widely, especially to Europe where he was able to see at first hand the contemporary practice on all the major continental railways, and had come in contact with the managers of most locomotive manufacturing firms. Whilst visiting Hungary, he became interested in the use of petrol engines to power rail vehicles. He made this field his special interest, persuading Ivatt to experiment with steam and petrol railmotors between Hatfield and Hertford. He also became acquainted with the firetube superheater which Wilhelm Schmidt had patented in Germany. It was whilst at Doncaster that Ivatt personally introduced Marsh as a new member of the Association of Railway Locomotive Engineers to sit amongst the elite conclave of locomotive engineers. Later he is recorded in the *Proceedings of the I Mech E* as contributing to a discussion following a Paper in 1910 by George Hughes of the Lancashire & Yorkshire Railway (L&YR) on superheating. The Schmidt superheater had made its debut in this country on two goods engines of the L&YR, so equipped by the latter in 1906.

Appointment to Brighton

On 10th October, 1904, Mr William Rose, one of the Directors of the London Brighton & South Coast Railway, visited Robert Billinton 'when he found his condition to be very grave and that he quite recognises the impossibility of being able to retain the post of Locomotive and Carriage Superintendent beyond end of the present year'. The Brighton Board meeting on the 19th noted 'the disturbing circumstances of Mr Billinton's case and regretting the impending loss of his valuable service, accepted his resignation and invited formal applications for the post'.

They also asked the General Manager, William Forbes, to report upon the present organisation of the Locomotive, Carriage and Wagon Department. This information was in their hands on the 2nd November. L.S. Smart was manager of the locomotive construction branch (he left for a South African Railway in February 1905), A H. Panter was general foreman of the carriage and wagon works and was appointed manager of the carriage and wagon construction branch, John Richardson was outdoor superintendent to the chief superintendent of the running branch of the Department with James Brigden, outdoor foreman, appointed foreman of gas and water arrangements, while the key locomotive superintendents at New Cross and Battersea were E.W. Trangmar and John Archer respectively. This was essential information to place before the candidates as all of these officers attached to the company's locomotive, carriage and wagon superintendent were subject to his authority and control.

Marsh's previous acquaintance with Brighton must certainly been a factor in his submitting his application and a shortlist of names was laid before the Board who instructed the Secretary to request Messrs Cook, Drummond, Luard and Marsh to meet the Board on the 9th November. When that meeting convened, it was recorded that Robert Billinton had died two days earlier, 'a great sense of loss sustained at the death of an esteemed and valued officer who had occupied a responsible position in the company for nearly 15 years with conspicuous ability and success'.

There was an immediate urgency to give consideration to the appointment of a successor and the candidates were severally seen by the Board and the subject adjourned to a week later. It was then announced that Mr Douglas Earle Marsh had been appointed from the 1st January, 1905 at a commencing salary of £1,500 with charge of construction and maintenance of rolling stock and all other work hitherto dealt with in the Department. He was also to act in an advisory capacity over the design of new ships and the machinery, heavy repairs or renewals. Three sub-clauses referred to three months' notice, the company's entitlement to use free of charge all patents or improvements obtained or made by the superintendent and to follow previous practice with regard to apprentices, not more than four articled pupils taken on at any time (the first part of this latter clause being amended and taken out according to the minutes of 23rd November, Marsh possibly having his own ideas on the matter of apprenticeships). In fact on 17th May it was upped to six, with a maximum premium to cover five years fixed at £50, and favour to be shown to unindentured apprentices drawn from the sons of men in the service of the company.

Fortunately Ivatt had returned from his break in Italy just in time to receive a telegram from Marsh saying that he had accepted the job of CME on the LB&SCR and could he start on 1st January? It is said that Ivatt finished his lunch, and enjoyed the remainder of his leave as though nothing had happened!

Of incidental interest, the Drummond amongst the other candidates was not Dugald who was firmly in charge of the much larger London & South Western Railway (LSWR) Locomotive Department, but brother Peter who, not long afterwards, landed the locomotive superintendence of the Highland Railway. Typical of the thrifty Scotsman was a letter received on 7th December asking for the return of his testimonials and payment of £3 5s. expenses on the occasion of his interview!

A week later, the Board gave consideration to the advisability of appointing a Committee of the Board to deal specially with the business of the Locomotive and Carriage Department, instructing their Secretary accordingly and stipulated that proposals for the renewal of rolling stock be made each half-year and any important matters relating thereto be circulated amongst the Directors at least 10 days before meeting. It was also recorded that Marsh had applied to contribute to the company's Pension Fund. It would appear that pretty well everything had been buttoned up for Marsh to take the helm at Brighton.

Portrait of Douglas Earle Marsh.

The possibility of electrification was very much on the agenda prior to Marsh's coming and came to fruition on the South London Line during his superintendence. A three-coach train bound for London Bridge is captured passing through Grove tunnel near Denmark Hill.

A 'Crystal Palace' electric set awaits departure from Victoria, the headcode '1' denoting Crystal Palace. The angle chosen by the photographer portrays the rebuilt Victoria to good effect with a full array of enamelled advertisements up to roof level and a bare minimum of platform furniture so as not to impede the hordes of daily commuters. Most of the electrical equipment came from AEG in Germany and, as a result of the outbreak of hostilities, the electrification programme came to an abrupt halt during World War I. Little attempt was made to design an attractive driver's front end, adapting a standard coach with two windows either side of a central headcode indicator. *Author's Collection*

Chapter Two

Innovations

As Marsh took stock of the Locomotive Department's requirements, he quickly found himself in agreement with the thinking within the Locomotive Committee. On 1st March he reported to the Board that the number of locomotives now requiring repair was abnormal. He proposed to discontinue locomotive building at Brighton and to concentrate the whole of the staff on repair work during the year. A sub-committee of Messrs Cardew, Macrae, Milburn and Sir Spencer Walpole was set up to consider the whole question of repair and renewal of the locomotive stock. Meanwhile Marsh was to proceed with repairs as rapidly as possible. There was a need for larger more powerful locomotives for express services to catch up with the heavier loadings of the new eight-wheel rolling stock and the same held to a lesser degree for the main line's goods services. He rapidly realised that new designs were needed to regularise the locomotive situation. However, there were more pressing areas of motive power that required urgent attention.

Electrification

In the inner suburbs of the metropolis, the company was experiencing intense competition from electric tramways which were luring away the public, especially those who lived a fair distance from their nearest suburban station and were happy to board a tram within a short distance from their front door. As C. Hamilton Ellis phrased it, 'the railway companies suddenly found them clanging off with a million of their regular passengers. If the trams did not pass one's front gate, one was probably to be found at the corner'. Marsh's aim was therefore to compete with the rapidly improving means of road transport by working a frequent service with a highly mobile and easily reversible combination.

The response to this threat lay in electrification, which, though not in Marsh's immediate orbit, nevertheless concerned him in detail. In 1903, the year of the first electrification of a British steam line, namely the Mersey Railway on the third rail system, Philip Dawson, an eminent electrical engineer and specialist in traction was asked to submit a report. He studied developments on the New York subway and in Italy. Dawson handed in his report in July 1904, and was instructed by the Brighton company to prepare specifications and call for tenders for the conversion of the South London line round from Victoria to London Bridge which was suffering most from a downturn on which passenger traffic had halved.

There followed simultaneously, much to Dawson's regret, a 'battle of systems' in which the single phase with overhead collectors eventually won the day. He was influenced by what had been seen in Italy, and in Major Cardew had an influential ally on the LB&SC Directorate. The tender of AEG Berlin was

The new LB&SCR steam railcar No. 1, completed in August 1905. The location may well be on the set of lines used by Beyer, Peacock & Co. for official photographs, taken not only for their own records but for illustrating their advertising catalogues. It and its companion introduced the Walschaert's valve gear to the Brighton Locomotive Department.

The scene is Brighton Works yard where last minute adjustments are being made to steam Railmotor No. 1, possibly for one of the trial trips. The power unit was built by Beyer, Peacock and the 48-seat coachwork was by the Electric Railway & Tramway Carriage Works of Preston. The railmotors proved capable of speeds of up to 60 mph on the level.   *R.C. Riley Collection*

accepted. It was over the technical design of the stock that Marsh became involved, Dawson devising the bow collectors in collaboration with Marsh.

The first experimental run took place on 17th January, 1909. Marsh was able to report 'Satisfactory trials of a train, worked by electric power on the South London Line between Battersea Park and East Brixton'. The public service was introduced on the 1st December. In the first year the new trains had more than doubled the number of passengers using steam traction in the previous 12 months (54 per cent in the first month and 125 per cent in December and had retrieved 4 per cent of its capital outlay), and by 1922 the stations on the line were serving 12 million passenger journeys a year, the public having been convinced by improved frequency, acceleration, cleanliness and comfort. Other LB&SCR London suburban lines were to follow using the overhead system. Such was the initial success that as early as the 3rd August, 1910 the Board was contemplating electrification of the main line, ordering a survey by AEG Berlin at their cost and without obligation on electrifying right through to Brighton, at the same time signing a contract worth £30,566 for a new depot at Selhurst, pointing the way to the future, decades ahead of their time.

Steam Railcars

Out in the country, lines and branches that had been patronised enthusiastically by the LB&SCR to fend off territorial threat from neighbouring rivals were now producing disappointing traffic returns, hardly warranting a train of three or four coaches. It was a question of economy, of retaining frequent services yet reducing on excessive payloads and accompanying fuel consumption, and Marsh was on the lookout for more economic power units.

During the mid-Edwardian period nearly all the major railway companies of any consequence were looking at steam railcars as the possible answer to turn round their loss making lines. To quote Hamilton Ellis, 'Steam rail motors were all the rage'. The Brighton Directors were certainly forward looking in this respect and considered all possible options. By the time of Marsh's arrival they already had a fund of experience gained on the East Southsea branch, which was jointly owned by the LSWR and the LB&SCR. A pair of steam railcars had been built to Dugald Drummond's design and introduced into service in 1903 in an attempt to make the branch pay its way. Marsh's predecessor, Robert Billinton, had been monitoring their performance and was asked to investigate further on the possibilities. The report in early 1904 favoured steam railcars against petrol railcars, but the Board after receiving Dawson's report favouring the latter held back, and then opted for both types.

The steam railcars were supplied by Beyer, Peacock & Co. to similar dimensions to a pair of cars being assembled for the North Staffordshire Railway at a cost, with minor modifications, of £2,145, and arrived just over a week after the petrol cars. Numbered 1 and 2 in a separate railcar list, the units had an all-over cab from which only the smokebox and chimney emerged. The engines had single driving wheels, Walschaert's valve gear, outside cylinders, Belpaire fireboxes, locomotive-type boilers and steam braking. The water

Steam railcar No. 1 on trial between Brighton and Eastbourne on 31st August 1905, and seen east of Lewes - the water crane at the end of the yard is visible on the left. The set of signals on view comprise the Lewes East home and the Southerham down distant for the lines to Eastbourne and Seaford respectively. The large white gap to the left of the railcar has not been caused by steam or smoke but is part of the chalk down backcloth of Malling and Cliffe Hill.

R.C. Riley Collection

A delightful postcard shows steam railcar No. 1 entering the easternmost track into Eastbourne station. In the background stands Messrs Beeney's warehouse used for storing grain, formerly the site of the Eastbourne Electric Lighting Company. The building was destroyed by enemy action in 1943.

THE STEAM MOTOR CAR
Running between Eastbourne and
St. Leonards.

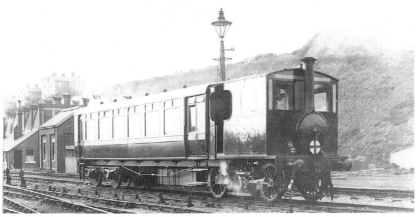

Steam railcar No. 2 stands outside St Leonard's shed. The original complex was rebuilt in 1898 to provide a modern shed which lasted through to the end of steam. The railcar service terminated at St Leonard's West Marina station, the SECR not permitting railmotors on their line into Hastings on the grounds of traffic congestion through the tunnels.

supply was carried in tanks below the carriage bodies, the latter sub-contracted to the Electric Railway & Carriage Works of Preston. There were slight differences in the accommodation arrangements of the two vehicles. The controls in the rear driving compartment operated those on the footplate through rodding in the roof, but for greater convenience were later resited under the carriage.

In their favour over the petrol cars was smooth riding at speed, ease of maintenance, speeds of 50 mph were well within their compass, but one minus was a tendency, due to lack of adhesion, to slip in unfavourable weather. Trials took place on the coast lines west and east of Brighton prior to commencing on the intensive 26 return journey service between Eastbourne and St Leonards in September 1905, and continuing through to the summer of 1912 when the limited passenger capacity could no longer cope with the holiday traffic. In 1913 they were transferred on to the Woodside-Selsdon Road shuttle but were soon laid aside. Then in the spring of 1918 they were used on temporary lines to the Thames Ammunition Works near Erith before being sold the next year for service in Trinidad.

Petrol Cars

The Brighton Directors were sufficiently innovative to seek a report on the new forms of traction that were emerging both in this country and Europe, and Philip Dawson, Consulting Engineer, submitted his report dated 21st April, 1904 on the use of Automobiles on Railways, his brief being to examine the relative merits of electric, steam and petrol cars. Electric accumulator cars had

A close comparison of the differences is afforded by these photographs of petrol cars Nos. 3 and 4, both taken at Kemp Town. The cars were originally provided with gangways so that they could run in tandem, but the end gates were dispensed with and fully glazed ends provided.

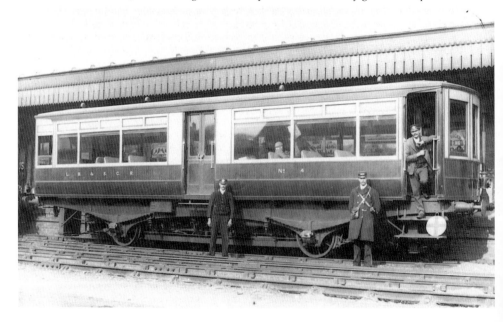

so far proved generally unsatisfactory 'because of the heavy costs of maintenance, repairs, renewal of batteries and low efficiency, and those still running (in Italy and Germany) are shortly to be taken off'. Regarding steam cars he reminded the Directors, 'You have been experimenting . . . between Fratton and Southsea using an ordinary type of locomotive' also referring to similar ventures on the Taff Vale Railway and in France. 'The results leave much to be desired, especially over costs of repairs and renewals, and the whole unit having been laid aside for considerable periods for cleaning and repairing purposes.'

Regarding petrol cars, these came in two types; the petrol engine driving an electric generator, being experimented with on the North Eastern Railway (NER), but over which there were problems with gearing and costs; the other involved direct mechanical transmission from motors to car wheels, and almost every point was in its favour. 'There is no doubt that the petrol engines pure and simple with ordinary gearing, both for reversing and changing speeds, is the most practical method at present in existence'. Dawson noted various examples on four European Railways and that the Great Northern Railway (GNR) was having two constructed. 'There is a field for motor cars on lines of light traffic.'

His recommendation was to advise buying petrol cars and place a trial order with Messrs Dick, Kerr & Co. (of Preston) 'who are at present constructing some petrol cars fitted with Coventry/Daimler motors for the GNR'. The Brighton Board considered the report on three separate occasions before deciding on the 8th June, 1904 to put things on hold till the current trials on the NER between steam and petrol railcars had been completed and reported upon. The findings appeared in Marsh's in tray on 3rd January, 1905, having been almost the very first matter requiring his attention following his assuming the locomotive superintendence at Brighton. He had little need to brief himself since he had been closely involved, having made this field his special interest and encouraged Ivatt in this direction. Brailsford mentions that Marsh was a great motoring enthusiast, owning his own car and enjoyed tinkering with petrol engines.

The Brighton Directors however, preferred to keep an open mind regarding the merits of steam and petrol cars and plumped for a brace of each. They preferred Dick, Kerr & Co.'s higher estimate by £200 over Kerr, Stuart & Co.'s £1,975 because the former were prepared to deliver them on six month trial and accept them back at £2,000 if found mechanically unsatisfactory. The relevant Board Minute for the 8th March, 1905 reads: 'A Petrol Rail Motor Car to be set up at the expense of the Contractors and lent to the Company for experimental purposes between Brighton and the Dyke, working expenses except fuel and operating materials to be borne by the contractor who will supervise working'. They built the bodywork, the mechanical parts being added to by the Daimler Car Co. at New Cross, and were completed in August 1905 as Nos. 3 and 4. Common features were two 35 hp four-cylinder Daimler engines, close seating for 48 passengers in reversible seats in two saloons with a central vestibule, running on four wheels thanks to the light weight of 17¾ tons. They differed in appearance as No. 3 had a clerestory roof and side windows divided into lower and upper panes, No. 4 had an arc roof and single panes. Both were painted in the coaching livery of umber and cream.

Taken from the platform end at Brighton terminus, this rare, slightly faded, picture of both petrol cars together finds them located between Brighton West signal box (120 levers) on the left and the much larger Brighton South box of 240 levers. The body of car No. 4 stands set up on stilts while its wheels have been removed for mechanical attention.

Photographs of the petrol cars on the move are few and far between. This delightful cameo depicts car No. 3 departing from St Leonard's West Marina station. In the background new Edwardian housing stands on the high ground overlooking the tunnel into Hastings at Bopeep Junction.   *R.C. Riley Collection*

No. 4 was the first to be delivered and given a test run from New Cross to Redhill, followed by No. 3, which was run on the Guildford branch. No. 4 then ran trials on the level line between Eastbourne and St Leonard's, joined by No. 3 when 'motor' services commenced between these two stations on 14th September, 1905. To capture additional traffic six unstaffed halts were opened along the line for easier access to the many excellent beaches along this stretch of the coast. Described in the Board Minutes as 'Wayside platforms', they were to be set up at Glyne Gap, Collington Wood, Cooden Golf, Pevensey Sluice and Pevensey Bay at a cost of £2,400. Earlier in June Marsh had discussions with the builders regarding a more powerful version using two 55 hp engines for use on the steeply graded Dyke branch. A similar type car was to run on loan from Dick, Kerr & Co. for experimental purposes on the Dyke Railway, but was then required by the GNR and the arrangement cancelled. Construction was authorised for this experimental car for £700 at Brighton works, but such specialised work proved beyond the resources of the erecting shop. Marsh was later forced to cancel the project although that December he had supervised trials with a Hungarian-designed steam car which, according to Bradley, 'failed dismally climbing to the Dyke, causing disillusion and Marsh to drop any further experimentation with railcars', although the Southern Railway came back to the idea in 1933 with a Sentinel Rail Bus which worked for periods over the branch with limited success.

The two petrol cars were constantly stopped for mechanical attention, and unpopular with crew and passengers on account of severe vibration and exhaust fumes. They were insufficiently powered, difficult to start, had to work excessively in low gear, became overheated and stalled frequently. When Marsh was asked to report to the Locomotive Committee comparative costs and fuel consumption per mile between steam railcars, petrol railcars, a 'Terrier' and a 'D' tank, the 'Terrier' won hands down on all counts and was to turn Marsh's mind in the direction of 'Terrier'-hauled 'Motor Trains'. The petrol cars took over the Kemp Town branch at the start of 1906 with 29 return journeys scheduled daily,

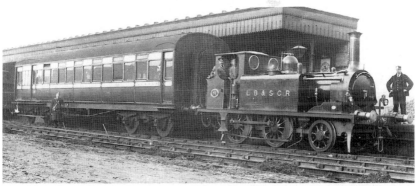

As early as December 1905 trials were conducted by Marsh using 'Terrier' No. 81 which had been converted to a 2-4-0T fitted with motor gear that September. The success of this experiment spelt the demise of the railcars and the widespread introduction by Marsh of separate locomotive and trailer combinations on sparsely patronised services.

The newly-constructed Ham Bridge Halt viewed in August 1905. There are still some finishing touches to be done prior to its opening for motor train traffic on 3rd September. At that time the coastal area west of Hove was largely given over to market gardening, but the owners of glasshouses obviously went in for honey too.   *H.C.P. Smail Collection/Bluebell Archives*

By this date in the post-World War I period Ham Bridge Halt has weathered somewhat. On view are the shelter, wooden access ramp and a fine array of station oil lamps, as a motor-fitted 'D1', sandwiched between a pair of two-coach push-pull sets introduced in 1912, calls at the up platform.   *H.C.P Smail Collection/Bluebell Archives*

Marsh deciding they could be more advantageously employed there than alongside the steam railcars on the Eastbourne-St Leonard's route. Authorisation was given for the construction of Hartington Road Halt on that branch. To service the railcars an inspection pit with screen to form a solid shed was ordered to be constructed at Brighton station at a cost of £730. Certain modifications followed at Brighton works before they were moved in October to the Lewes-Seaford services, but further mechanical failures in 1908 caused both to be more powerfully re-engined in the winter of 1909/10 at the expense of increased vibration and petrol consumption. However, 'Terriers' were frequently summoned to stand in as in one final instance where the railcar froze up in Kemp Town tunnel, according to Hamilton Ellis, 'full of angry and influential passengers for the 8.45 am City Limited'. As a result the General Manager ordered them both to be taken out of service in 1911, and be removed from Running Stock and placed as Service Stock in the Electrical Department for use in inspecting and repairing overhead wiring, where they survived until 1928.

Motor Trains (Push-pull)

Neither sets of railcars could cope with seasonal traffic fluctuations nor had they sufficient power to haul an additional trailer that a 'Terrier' could handle with comfort. The experiment with both types of railcar had not been successful enough to progress in either direction. However Marsh had been brave enough to innovate, assess and examine the possibilities, learn from them and come up with something still better.

Marsh was looking for a greater degree of flexibility to provide for increased passenger loadings and, as a result of the aforementioned trials, which took place in September 1905, 'Terrier' No. 81 *Beulah* with its trailer car, or sometimes a pair, had the edge over its rivals by a wide margin in almost every respect. While all four competing railcars were stopped for 14 or more days, the 'Terrier' incurred no failure in traffic. Marsh reported the operating costs to the Locomotive Committee who agreed to equip more 'Terriers' and some 'D' tanks with motor train gear and authorised the construction of 15 improved trailer cars at a cost of £750 each for various lines noted for lightly loaded services. Indeed, that August the General Manager had drawn attention to 'the growing competition of the tramway and motor omnibuses which run between Worthing and Brighton, and reported that with the use of a trailer car worked by 'A' class engines with the provision of halts, a useful service could be established to increase the passenger takings'. The Board ordered halts at Holland Road, Dyke Junction, Fishergate, Kingston and Ham Bridge at a cost of £1,230, the service to start as soon as possible.

No. 232 was the first 'D' tank to be fitted with motor train equipment in November 1905, followed by Nos. 605 and 627 in 1909, serving between them the Horley to Horsham and Epsom Downs to West Croydon services. From 1910 through to the 1923 Grouping another 61 of the class were converted to motor working, at first with the locomotive sandwiched between two trailer cars with driving compartments at either end of the train, but later adapted to two-car push-pull sets.

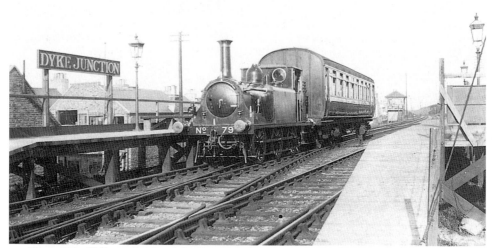

'Terrier' No. 79 (formerly *Minories*) calls at Dyke Junction with a Brighton to Worthing railmotor in 1908. It was some years before motor trains were used up to the Dyke following the fitting of motor train equipment to the more powerful 'D' class 0-4-2Ts.

M.P. Bennett Collection/Bluebell Archives

This posed photograph taken during the layover at Kemp Town shows the 'Terrier' and 'Balloon' motor train to perfection. 'A1' class 0-6-0T No. 643 (formerly *Gipsyhill*) was one of a set slated in the 1905-6 withdrawal programme but reprieved by Marsh to carry motor gear for working the new motor train services. Coach No. 1329 was one of the second batch of 'Balloon' trailers built in 1906.   *Author's Collection*

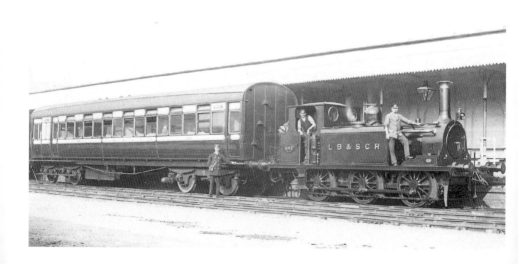

To quote the late Handel Kardas 'the Brighton philosophy was not so much to replace existing services as to use the "motors" to increase service frequency. This was done in urban areas to compete with the frequent and cheap road transport and on rural lines to meet the demands for more trains at a low cost.'

At first the remote control gear was purely mechanical, the regulator handle being moved by a series of push rods and slides but was later replaced by an electro-pneumatic compressed air system, fed from the Westinghouse equipment. First to benefit were the nearby suburbs of Brighton and Kemp Town, Hove and the villages stretching towards the Dyke which came to enjoy a frequent service previously unknown to them in the days when delay from set trains changing engines at each terminal or running round was the mode of operation. The Kemp Town branch witnessed a 77 per cent increase in passengers, the traffic to the Dyke 20 per cent. Their success was quickly apparent and within two years Marsh had extended the use of motor trains to other parts of the system including beyond Worthing to Littlehampton, Hayling Island and Seaford branches and to local services around Horsham, Three Bridges, East Grinstead, Oxted and Tunbridge Wells with halts proposed in the latter area at Ruspur Road Crossing, Roffey Crossing, Lyons Crossing, High Rocks, Hurst Green and Monks Bridge. They operated between Chichester and Portsmouth, where halts were authorised at Fishbourne, Nutbourne, Southbourne and Bedhampton at a cost of £850, and up in the London suburbs between West Croydon and Belmont, and Tooting, Merton and Wimbledon, working to and from Streatham. With growing requirements for this field of traffic, Marsh, as will be seen, further improved the Stroudley 'Terriers' so that on lightly graded lines they were able to take an extra trailer, thus pointing the way forward. Marsh's rail motor combination proved so successful that two decades later the new Southern Railway adopted it in general use from end to end of the widespread system. Motor push-pull services were to remain a common feature until the penultimate years of steam operation.

The 'Terriers' obviously had something to spare and sometimes ran not only propelling a 'Balloon' coach but, as in this case , hauling an additional six- wheeled brake third, here seen passing Balham Intermediate box *en route* to West Croydon.

This photograph of Ivatt 'C1' class Atlantic No. 276 serves to portray the great similarities between the Ivatt and Marsh Atlantics. Apart from the external differences mentioned in the text, the Marsh version had the piston stroke lengthened by two inches and the working pressure raised from 175 to 200 lb. per sq. in.

The first Marsh Atlantic No. 37 stands outside Littlehampton shed in works grey primer, and is the focus of interest from both staff and passengers standing on the platform opposite. A test run on 17th December, 1905 began the 1,000 mile trial period which extended into the following year, all prior to the application of the new umber livery, the lining being in gold with the splashers bare of any embellishment. Note the bogie brakes, auxiliary guard-irons, Derby-type chimney, flat-sided safety valve casing and makers' plates on leading section of frames.

R.C. Riley Collection

The Marsh Atlantics (Class 'H1')

Much has been written concerning Marsh's locomotives in numerous books and articles and it is not proposed to recapitulate the many technical facts which can be found in considerable detail, especially in D.L. Bradley's *Locomotives of the LB&SCR* that can hardly be improved upon in scope. This chapter rather looks at the thinking behind Marsh's locomotive programme, their performance during his regime and an assessment of what was achieved before later engineers tinkered further with those which underperformed, and finally seeks to place developments in the context of his reign at Brighton.

In discussing the origins and thinking behind the Atlantics, Bradley suggests that Marsh was looking for a 'quick fix' to regularise the locomotive position, as a complete new design would have taken up valuable time that was at a premium. Marsh had been closely involved on his arrival at Doncaster with the creation of Ivatt's pioneering Atlantic design, where trailing axles, in the words of Roger Hennessey, author of the book *Atlantic*, supported fireboxes which generated plenty of horsepower in order to maintain high speeds for long periods. The outward sign of their water boiling capacity was the wide firebox - 'a cavernous chamber,' an idea Marsh may have brought from broad-gauge Swindon. The go-ahead came from the Engine Stock Committee meeting on 22nd March, 1905. Marsh made the case, stressing the increase in the weight of trains, especially now that Victoria station was being rebuilt with lengthened platforms, with the demand for an acceleration in speed 'necessitating provision of engines of a more powerful type than those at present in use on the railway'. Marsh had come from a large engine line and he went on to produce a photograph of an engine of the Atlantic type now in use on the Great Northern Railway which could haul 400 ton trains as opposed to the 'B' type's 300 tons. He proposed to abolish the class 'B' bogie type as obsolete, recommending the construction of five of the Atlantic type at approximately £4,000 each. The Committee authorised him to proceed and prepare specifications and drawings and invite tenders. A week later the Board approved the order.

Time was of the essence, hence the resort to the 'Doncaster drawings'. It is said that Ivatt allowed Marsh to take the drawings of the large Atlantic with him to Brighton, perhaps out of recognition that Marsh had been chief assistant mechanical engineer and works manager at Doncaster and closely involved with the design of the GNR '251' class large boiler Atlantics.

Certainly it was arranged for a complete set of the original working drawings to be made available to Brighton. There they were modified to comply with LB&SC requirements, being annotated in red ink. The 36 page specification with amended drawings and tendering documentation was dispatched early April. In view of the locomotive repair backlog, the order went to outside tender, the last LB&SCR engines built other than at Brighton. The quote of Messrs James Kitsons of the Arndale Foundry at Leeds of £3,950 per engine was accepted on the 19th April, the price being reduced three weeks later by £45 each if delivered in grey primer. Marsh was in a hurry to see these engines on the road and slipped in a clause entitling Kitsons to a premium of £10 per week if delivery

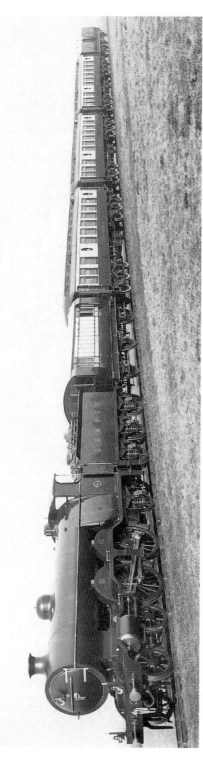

Above: The three Pullmans pictured in this official photograph on the Crumbles ballast branch outside Eastbourne, *Princess Patricia, Princess Ena* and *Duchess of Norfolk* are in fact contemporaneous with Atlantic No. 38. Dating from 1906, these were the last 'British' cars to be built in the USA, being shipped in knocked-down form for re-assembly at the LB&SCR's Brighton works. Although posed here as a set, these cars were intended to be worked singly and could not originally be gangwayed together to provide through access. They were the first Pullmans to be finished in the umber-and-cream livery.

Fred Stone Memorial Collection/Bluebell Archives

Right: In June 1907 No. 39, suitably equipped with an indicator shelter at the front end for its recorders, one of whose caps can just be discerned above the parapet, ran a set of trial runs on the 'Brighton Limited' Pullman express on the Brighton main line. On the last day of that month the Atlantic achieved 86½ mph near Wivelsfield and made the 50.9 miles to Brighton in 51 mins 48 sec. The photographer, Wentworth S. Gray has captured the train near Star Lane, south of Coulsdon.

was effected a week or weeks before the stipulated date. When delivered between 10th December, 1905 and 10th February, 1906, it only remained for the Brighton to connect them up, and this was carried out in the paint shop where upon assembly they were conveniently painted in running colours. When first registered in the Locomotive Register they were shown under class 'B5' but in February 1906 changed to 'H Atlantic' and 'H1' on 1st January, 1907.

Ever since debate has raged as to the degree of imitation of the GNR design. Ben Webb is clear: 'a copy of Ivatt's Great Northern type'. Maskelyne: 'practically identical with Ivatt's Atlantic'. Dr Ian Allen maintains: 'the Marsh Atlantics Nos. 37-41 cannot be considered an original class'. R.N. Hardy more cautiously writes, 'Doncaster drawings were used as the basis so that the final product had much in common with the Ivatt Atlantics' and this is probably nearer the truth. They differed externally from the GNR Atlantics in the following respects: a more artistic Billinton-type chimney, a larger cab with longer roof supported at the rear corners by pillars, more rounded tops to the dome cover and a continuous curved footplate. The 'B4'-type tender had coal rails that only extended three-quarters of the way back from the cab ends.

They had deeper fireboxes and 18½ in x 26 in. cylinders compared to the smaller diameter cylinders of the GNR Atlantics, and with a tractive effort 3,000 lb. greater than the Doncaster counterparts, were briskly away from a standing start. Marsh's deep wide firebox was a throwback from Swindon, Ivatt on the drawings, later 'borrowed' by Marsh, of his larger Atlantics had annotated 'BG Firebox', possibly at Marsh's instigation as photographs in the Firefly Trust's collection feature several of the splendid broad-gauge creations of Daniel Gooch with their large fireboxes which certainly had made a great impression upon Marsh during his time at Swindon. The 5 ft 6 in. diameter boilers were by far the largest that had appeared on the LB&SCR up to that time. Also significant was the raising of the boiler pressure from 175 to 200 lb./sq. in., whilst the stroke of the pistons was lengthened by two inches. The 'H1s' were fitted with air-assisted screw reversing gear carried on an enormous casting on top of which the driver perched himself whereas the Ivatt engine's driver stood at his work most of the time. The gear relied for ease of operation from air in the Westinghouse system, which was mounted vertically between the frames. The footplate continued over the cylinders unlike the Ivatts. The greater distance behind the trailing axle was usefully employed to gain a more commodious cab and footplate. Each locomotive had two pairs of cased Ramsbottom safety valves atop the firebox. Apart from these differences, not all overtly visible, the engines might have come straight out of Doncaster works.

With their large free steaming boilers and wide fireboxes, they appeared reasonably successful. R.N. Hardy submits that 'it was the higher pressure that made the difference and I have no doubt that in their original form, the five LB&SCR engines were quicker off the mark and just as free running as their saturated GN contemporaries'. With this Bradley is in agreement describing them as 'notably lively with good acceleration with the heavier loads than the 'H2s' as they were fitted with balanced slide valves. These were the Richardson type used in the USA on many of the contemporary outside-cylindered locomotives with the steam chest above the cylinders. The back of the slide valve was built up with

No. 37 at its first repaint received monograms featuring the company's initials intertwined on all splashers, earning the nickname 'raspberries'. With its lightly loaded train of six-wheeled stock on a running-in duty following its repaint, it is seen passing Purley Downs Road *circa* 1909. In the distance stand the brand new houses of Edwardian Purley.   *Author's Collection*

Marsh Atlantic No. 41 powers a London Bridge to Brighton train south of Coulsdon, at one of Cecil Laundy's favourite photographic locations. Of particular interest is the leading coach, a 'Crystal Palace' motor third brake, heading south, possibly to Lancing for some major repair to its bodywork. Note that though the handsome LB&SCR monogram was retained on both driving splashers, the number, which formerly appeared on small brass plates, was now painted on the cab sides in line with the tender lettering.   *R.C. Riley Collection*

a chamber into which exhaust steam could enter through a ⅜ in. hole and this would keep the valve on the steam chest face irrespective of regulator opening'. This is questioned by Bert Perryman who maintains they were 'not the initial success that had been expected, unsuperheated, coupled with a 200 lb. sq. in. boiler pressure and somewhat under-cylindered'. However, the locomen always considered the 'H1s' to be freer-running locomotives.

The Marsh Atlantics were a gift to the publicity department at a time when most southern companies were firmly glued to the 4-4-0, compared to which these machines were giants. The Atlantics stole the show, looking superb in Marsh's umber livery and being maintained in top class condition. Eric Langridge recalls as a young apprentice, 'Marsh's version of the LB&SC monogram and umber shade of paint stick in my memory. The shape of the lettering and figures were very handsome indeed'. Derek Cross poses the question, 'Was the Brighton line suitable for a large boiler, wide firebox Atlantic?' He felt they were not the right type of locomotive for maximum journeys in the region of 50-70 miles and they never really got the chance to warm up; their 6 ft 7½ in. driving wheels were too large for the taxing climbs through the Downs. Like most Brighton engines they were built to last and proved a great step forward on what had gone before. The 'H1s' were fitted eventually with 24 element Schmidt superheaters by the Southern Railway between 1925-27 adding considerably to their potency, though Bert Perryman in Brighton works noted that their gunmetal balanced slide valves did not take kindly to superheated steam and rapidly became deeply scored.

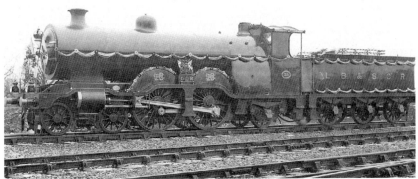

No. 39 was always considered a 'good' engine and came to be reserved for Royal and other important specials. In this capacity it conveyed Turkish VIPs from Portsmouth to Victoria c. 1908-9, and is suitably 'dressed overall'. In 1913 it was to acquire the name *La France* just prior to being used to haul the special on the occasion of the visit of the French President, M. Raymond Poincaré. The photograph was taken by Frank Burtt.

Atlantics Nos. 421 and 422 under construction in Brighton works during the spring of 1911, just prior to Marsh's resignation. At first the engines were classified 'H1/S' but later this was adjusted to 'H2'.

Official photograph taken on the Crumbles siding of the first 'H2' Atlantic painted slate grey and fully-lined out in black and white. It did not receive the umber livery until June 1913.

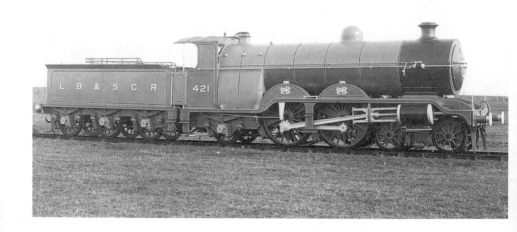

The Brighton Atlantics (Class 'H2')

Though Marsh had no direct part in their ordering and construction, the 'H2' Atlantics bear his print as an improved version of the 'H1'. Between February 1910 and March 1911 the locomotive drawing office had under his initial direction completed the majority of drawings for a superheated version of the 'H1s', benefiting from the design expertise of Basil Field, Marsh's chief draughtsman. Perryman is incorrect in assuming that they must have been ordered by Marsh since they began to emerge as soon as June 1911. The fact is that when further express passenger locomotives became necessary in 1910, Marsh came up with his 'J' class 4-6-2 tank No. 325 which was still suffering with some teething troubles when he resigned. The Locomotive Committee agreed to play safe and in view of the huge backlog of repairs, despite the reorganisation of Brighton works and with Billinton's persuading the Board to agree to unlimited overtime being worked, on 4th April, 1911 ordered six superheated Atlantics from Brighton works, at first classified class 'H1/S' but later adjusted to 'H2' at a cost of £3,265 each.

They differed from the 'H1s' in superheating, with an unrivalled area of 479 sq. ft, a resultant lower 170 lb. sq. in. working pressure with advantage to boiler maintenance, in larger 21 in. x 26 in. cylinders, while the smokebox was carried on a supporting saddle. They had flared safety valve covers and 10 in. piston valves with a travel of $4^{11}/_{16}$ in. They carried a more shapely Marsh built-up parallel chimney, a straight footplate clearing the big outside cylinders, the majority of these features accounting for an increased weight of 30 cwt. The end result was a very powerful machine with a tractive effort of 20,800 lb. far in excess of the GN 'C1s': and to boot a locomotive of extreme elegance. J.N. Maskelyne comments: 'L. Billinton tidied up the external details, substituting a chimney of his own design, extending the cab roof 15 in. to the rear pillars, and smoothed the run of footplating which in the Marsh engines contrived to reach five different levels in its progress from front to back of engine.' Instead of gilt, yellow paint was used in the lining and a new coat of arms replaced the company's monogram.

They proved an instant success. Locomen took to them at once, and standards of performance were high. They registered an economy on coal of upwards of 10 per cent compared with the 'H1s'. They were good easy riding engines and 'at work on a stiff grade there was no noise, no hustle, just a steady strong pull all the way', testified Derek Cross. Drivers said they always seemed to respond at once to the first touch of the regulator, and recovered well from signal checks and speed restrictions for curves, both common features on the Brighton's system. If they had a fault they were deficient in adhesion in adverse weather and there were instances of stalling on the 1 in 64 climb out of Victoria, requiring rear assistance.

Various modifications were undertaken by the Southern Railway (SR), which further improved the class. Vacuum ejectors were fitted in 1924, rail washing apparatus in 1933, and in 1936 the boiler pressure was raised to 200 lb. sq. in. to standardise the 'I2' boilers used between both Atlantic classes. Between 1934 and 1938 the Schmidt superheaters were replaced by Maunsell's version as a final development while at this same period they were altered to the SR's composite loading gauge. Interestingly enough both classes on average achieved the same life span of some 45 years and served the LB&SCR and its successors with distinction.

Before leaving the Atlantics it is worth asking the question as to Marsh's wisdom in launching out into Atlantics at the end of the 'bull market', despite the need for a quick fix for more effective motive power for the express traffic, for the LB&SCR was last but one in the field in Great Britain to adopt this wheel arrangement. The term 'Atlantic' came from North America which, with its wide open expanses, quickly took the lead in constructing large locomotives incorporating an ever increasing number of wheels under the engine. In Britain the type was not taken up in any significant numbers. Opinion suggests that Marsh with a little more patient foresight might have been wiser to use six-coupled express engines from the start. Indeed it is said that the mind of his predecessor, Robert Billinton, was revolving around the idea for 4-6-0 engines. It came as no surprise that the GWR rebuilt 15 of its 4-4-2s as 4-6-0s within a few years of their construction, and the majority of the type in the country had gone to the breakers by the outbreak of World War II. Be that as it may, the last non-Brighton 4-4-2 was withdrawn at the end of 1950, leaving eight Brighton Atlantics to outlast them, No 32424 by almost eight years, a truly remarkable achievement when the main arteries of their home stamping ground had been electrified as, far back as the 1930s. The Bluebell Railway arrived just too late to preserve Atlantic No. 32424 *Beachy Head* but it is currently seeking to make amends by building an 'H2' using a surviving Ivatt Atlantic boiler.

Littlehampton shed in September 1911 with two Atlantics posed for the camera of F.W. Spry, a local photographer. 'H1' No. 38 appears in perfect condition, having had its beading thoroughly burnished, even on the front of the cab roof. The new 'H2' out of works that very month is on its trial run from Brighton works to Littlehampton and back, unidentified as yet with just '1502 a/c No. 3' chalked on its smokebox cover, later to be numbered 423. Its crew stand by together with a young works apprentice, possibly John Pelham Maitland.

The 'C3' Class 0-6-0

Immediately after the Atlantics Marsh turned his attention towards a new class of main line goods engine. Loads on the main line had outgrown the power of Robert Billinton's 'C2s' though the latter remained adequate for country branch line work. Hamilton Ellis suggests the 'C3' 'was in essentials a Billinton type and the styling was Billinton's too, but it had the first examples of the larger boiler used by Marsh with which he hoped to upgrade a whole set of Billinton classes'. Interestingly a Board Minute for 29th May urged the construction of 10 goods engines as an alternative to workmen in the Brighton shops being placed on short time or some even being discharged, the costs to be debited to the 1906 Revenue Account. Ordered in October, the 'C3s' were constructed at Brighton works during the following year at a cost of £2,380 each. The first two were laid down as Nos. 595 and 596 but before assembly had been changed to Nos. 300 and 301, the earlier numbers going to the 'I1s' on which building commenced later that year.

The time-honoured Stroudley regulator valve and elegant regulator handle were swept away in favour of the standard Great Northern pattern and Ramsbottom safety valves. Bradley describes the class as a 'strange mixture of Robert Billinton and Stroudley practice for, whereas the tender, smokebox, chimney and cylinders followed that of Marsh's predecessor, the actual brake rodding, duplex donkey pump, crosshead pumps and preheated feed-water from the tender where the temperature was raised by contact with the heat of exhaust steam, were reminiscent of Stroudley'. Cylinders were a smaller version of the pattern used on the 'E6' tanks, Robert Billinton having died before any of the 12 ordered had left Brighton works, and it was left to Marsh to see the class completed. The 'C3s' were paired to tenders holding four tons of coal and over 3,000 gallons of water. However the thinness of the metal rendered them prone to leaks and these were soon replaced with ones which lacked feedwater apparatus from the 'B2' class as they came to be rebuilt between 1908 and 1910. The engines were painted in Marsh's new lined-black livery with cabside numberplates, the great majority being first based at Brighton.

An interesting aside from the personal ledger in Gerard Collins' possession of the private records of George Aylwin, Stroudley's nominated driver for all trial trips, suggests Marsh had it in mind to design the 'C3s' originally as Compounds. 'From appearance this engine can only be a two cylinder compound.' Aylwin had long since retired from the footplate but obviously had many contacts with the works people. He may have picked this up by chatting with one of the Brighton draughtsmen. It is possible that Marsh had compounding in mind which would have been the subject of earlier draft drawings which were quickly discarded. Certainly the era was one of looking at compounding; Wordsell was building two-cylinder compounds on the NER and Ivatt, his former chief, built his large-boilered Atlantic No. 292 as a compound. The groundwork for this would have taken place during Marsh's supervision of the Doncaster drawing office, and he could well have come down to Brighton bringing the idea with him. Aylwin goes on to write 'I should say it's not much good for Goods working'.

The brand new pioneer 'C3' goods 0-6-0 No. 300 is transferred across from the works to Brighton shed for inaugural trials and test runs, in spite of the painting up being incomplete. The smokebox and front area is matt in sharp contrast with the shine of the rest of the locomotive. The photograph was taken in March 1906 by William Bennett.

M.P. Bennett Collection/Bluebell Archives

Another William Bennett coup - 'C3' No. 303 caught on a trial trip at Aldrington on the west coast line. Note the Special and Worthing headcode, the former status noted by the double diamond disc at the top of the smokebox. *M.P. Bennett Collection/Bluebell Archives*

Portrait of the pioneer 'C3' No. 300, probably taken on a trial run to Newhaven. The outline was similar to Robert Billinton's 'C2' class. In the words of Bradley: 'Although they looked the part, their performance was deplorable and the men found little good in them'. On the other hand upgraded No. 302 is seen in a fine F. Moore portrait on New Cross shed bearing the revised umber livery using yellow paint instead of gilt and the substitution of LBSC for the full LB&SCR.

Author's Collection

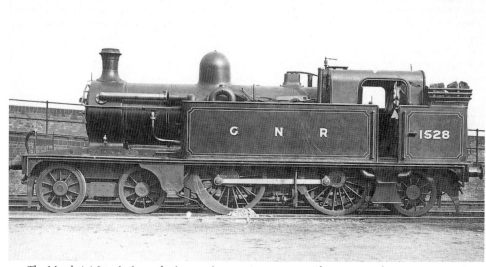

The Marsh 4-4-2 tank classes had many features in common with engines in the construction of which he had been closely involved at Doncaster works. An example of Ivatt's 'C12' class of 1898 shows the closeness in similarity of design to No. 595, the first of a long run of Atlantic tank engines. This engine initially differed from its successors in the arrangement of the feedwater heating pipes.

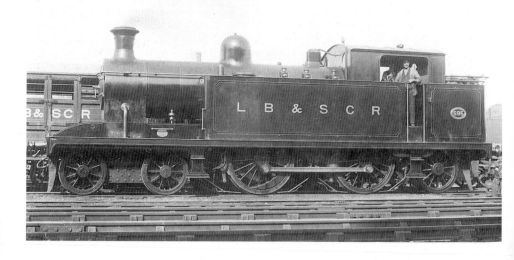

Bradley's pithy appraisal cannot be improved: 'Although they looked the part, their performance was deplorable and the men found little good in them'. Marsh was quick to realise their failings and made alterations to the firebox, grate and firebars, which increased the heating surface. The ashpan and dampers were modified and a circular extended smokebox was fitted. However they were never again an automatic main line choice, shed foremen much preferring the rebuilt 'C2xs' and the 'K' class as they became available.

Lawson Billinton, who succeeded Marsh, summarised their weaknesses: 'Poor acceleration because of the 17½ in. cylinders, outdated feed arrangement, the crosshead pumps were unable to keep the boiler up at low speeds and the massive boiler in reality offered similar heating surfaces to those of the C2s. Fuel consumption was extremely high'. Lawson Billinton tried to improve their performance by boring out the cylinders to 18 inches and fitting them with specially designed top-feed apparatus housed in a dome on the front ring, but to no avail. They were quickly found incapable of heavy main line work and relegated to less taxing duties. After the exigencies of World War I traffic when there was a call for all hands on deck, the majority gravitated to Horsham shed, confined to minor goods turns and occasional Sunday excursions, hence acquiring the nickname 'Horsham Goods'. Scrapping began in 1936 and only the outbreak of war brought a reprieve, the last member surviving until 1952.

What is surprising is that the brand new 'C3s' were so emphatically eclipsed by the rebuilt 'C2s' and this has never been fully explained. Hamilton Ellis ascribes the former as 'suffering the occultation of most less numerous classes of locomotive, the more extensive series lasting longer'. The 'C2xs' soldiered on for a good 10 years longer, a profitable investment right through to their final demise in 1962. With regard to the 'C3s' the 5 ft boiler, however, was not at fault and was used to advantage in rebuilding many of Billinton's small 4-4-0s and 0-6-0s and later Maunsell used it as a basis for the boiler of his 3-cylinder 0-8-0 tanks. As Dr Ian C. Allen stoutly maintained, 'Brighton boilers were second to none'.

The Atlantic Tanks

Marsh seems to have formed the idea that on a line on which the longest run was less than 80 miles, there should be plenty of scope for express passenger tank locomotives. He arrived from Doncaster with an ingrained preference for a leading bogie and, deeming the veteran 'D' tanks to be outclassed on both secondary and suburban services, went for a design based on Great Northern practice. His early 'I' class tanks were, according to A.B. McLeod, 'a complete crib of the GNR 4-4-2Ts, drawings of which Marsh borrowed from Doncaster'. During his regime he was to major on the Atlantic type tank with the leading bogie and pivoting axle. Marsh reintroduced condensing and increased water capacity by means of longer side tanks, which encroached into the cab; these were filled with baffle plates to counter surging. The deep cab side doors must have made the fireman's job a warm one, and as a result of complaints, Marsh called No. 595 in to be fitted with very elaborate roof ventilators. The cab boasted roof top clerestories with adjustable louvres and lagging - louvre deck would be a more accurate term for the accent was on ventilation rather than roof lighting.

This classic H. Gordon Tidey photograph shows the second 'I1' class, No. 596, on a down semi-fast from London Bridge to Brighton via Redhill south of Honor Oak Park. While the bowler-hatted figure in the cab - not Marsh surely? - seems aware of the photographer, the ganger on his 'walk' along the track appears oblivious.

A very grimy No. 2 on duty at Brighton station. While many of the Brighton's engines entered traffic in works grey and black due to logistical problems at Brighton works, No. 2 has not even got this far. The 'F' on the unpainted chimney denotes 'Front' for the information of fitters. Another of F. Moore's railway photographs.

The 'I1' Class

The new type was fitted with a standard Brighton 0-6-2 tank boiler which was derived from the Stroudley 'G' class single-wheeler of the 1880s. The first batch of 4-4-2Ts, Nos. 595-604, appeared between September 1906 and June 1907, by which time another 20 more had been ordered, but only 10 of these, Nos. 1-10, were built through to December 1907. These incorporated motion and fittings, coupled wheels, coupling rods, connecting rods and eccentric rods from Stroudley 'D1' and 'D2' locomotives which had been broken up, some have suggested, to ease Marsh's conscience since the 'Ds' could not legitimately be condemned on account of mechanical failure. Indeed the scrapping of the workmanlike 'Ds' was questioned by the Board who stipulated that these withdrawals should only continue if some serviceable parts were used in the new constructions. A more plausible reason was a reduction in cost of £323 on each locomotive at a time when penny pinching really counted, and this involved the batch in some dimensional changes. Indeed the 'I1s' were remarkable for many minor variations between individual engines, causing an old fitter in the erecting shop to remark that they were getting back to the Craven days when no two engines were alike. No. 595, in particular, differed from its successors with conspicuous condenser piping, flat-sided smokebox, a smooth cab roof and an 'E5'-type chimney.

The provision of condensing apparatus, a previous Stroudley practice discontinued by Billinton, was taken up by Marsh by dint of experience at Doncaster on Ivatt's 4-4-2 tank engines. In the case of No. 595 steam directed from the exhaust was taken through either side of the smokebox and conducted through copper tubes back along the side of the boiler and then down into the forward part of each side tank. In the rest of the class the pipes went downwards through the running plate and then bent round to reach the lower part of the side tanks.

Once out in full service they were soon found wanting in boiler power and feeble draughting. Charles Fryer suggests the diversion of the exhaust steam to condense in the tanks emasculated the blast, 'pulling its punch'. E.A. Langridge accounts for their poor steaming because the existing short coupling rods limited the length of the firebox and grate area. Hamilton Ellis in his critique writes, 'They were poor tools and their vice was in their boilers for they steamed badly. They were seen limping about the London suburban area'. Whatever the engine crews tried, writes Bradley, 'the result was the same, pitiful'. Apparently Marsh experienced their dismal performance at first hand for Lawson Billinton has described a day long struggle on the Royal Train from Victoria to Epsom Downs for the June 1907 Derby with both Marsh and himself on the footplate. Only a combination of skilful handling and good luck saw the new 'I' class No. 600 only just make the six mile gradient of 1 in 80 steepening to 1 in 63 from Hackbridge to Banstead. Edward VII was known to be a stickler for punctuality. The company was doubtless embarrassed to lose seven minutes on the outward journey and 11 on the return. These results led to a great deal of experiment with the chimney design and various modifications to the smokebox, and suitably placed baffle plates within the tanks to ensure that the heated water circulated better, but such marginal improvements prior to the 1922 Grouping came too late and too little. The new regime viewed them as an unwelcome

Royal Race Special near Banstead Downs hauled by 'I1' class No. 600. This three-month-old engine was specially prepared on Marsh's instructions in June 1907 for working the Royal Train to the Epsom Derby but, despite the presence of both Marsh and Lawson Billinton on the footplate, seven minutes were lost on the down journey struggling up the gradients and 11 on the return. This is one of several graphic photographs taken by E.T. Vyse at this location.

John Minnis Collection

The new 'I' tanks take over at Victoria. No. 1 heads a down Hastings excursion consisting of 14 Stroudley 4-wheeled coaches up Grosvenor Bank on 14th September, 1908. No. 3 has moved up from the platform end, shortly to drop back and couple up at the head of a later working. The photograph was taken by an electrification engineer seeking to make a case for his cause by proving that the smoke of steam locomotives obscured signals.   *R.C. Riley Collection*

Barely a month old, 'I2' No. 15 of May 1908 stands in mint condition at Epsom Downs at the head of the empty Royal Train to be photographed by Frank Burtt while everyone is occupied with the races. In addition to the Royal coat of arms, note the regal crown attached to the top of the smokebox. It was Brighton practice to allocate one of their latest engines for this prestige working Royal Train duty on Derby Day.

handicap, discounting their use on heavy suburban service duties. Thought was given to their withdrawal when the Brighton works manager suggested making use of boilers left spare by the rebuilds to class 'B4x' and the superheating of the saturated 'I3s'. All were rebuilt by Maunsell to class 'I1x' between July 1925 and February 1932 at Brighton works as heavy boiler repairs became necessary, incorporating some small modifications and raising the working pressure from 170 lb./sq. in. to 180 lb./sq. in. Even after this they were, as Hamilton Ellis succinctly phrased it 'decently useful' and survived on light rural services through to World War II and into the early years of Nationalisation.

The 'I2' and 'I4' Classes

With the alarm bells ringing over the performance of the 'I1s', the last 10 of the order for 20 was cancelled and 10 class 'I2s', Nos. 11 to 20, built in their place with larger 4 ft 6 in. boilers. The increased dimensions together with Field's newly designed cast-iron chimney and safety valve cover, flared out at the base, gave them a more imposing appearance which again sadly belied their performance and failed to live up to the excellent reputation of their Doncaster forebears or the Billinton radial tank. This was true also of the five 'I4' class locomotives of similar design fitted with superheated boilers. The 'I4s' owed their existence entirely to the economic use of a surplus set of late-delivered superheated boilers. Five superheated boilers ordered from the North British Locomotive Company (NBL) did not immediately materialise, so Marsh ordered five more replacements to be built at Brighton. When the NBL boilers did arrive in August 1908, they were used on five more 4-4-2Ts, Nos. 31-35, which

In the spring of 1908 the newly-built 'I2' No. 13 was taken out onto the Crumbles line for an official photograph taken by Frank Burtt. It was the general rule that engines scheduled to appear before the official photographer received a hurried temporary coat of grey, duly lined in white, only on the side facing the camera.

Opportunity was taken when photographing 'I2' class No. 13 on the Crumbles line to line it up next to 'D' tank No. 281 *Withyham*. The new Marsh Atlantic tanks were designed with the intention of replacing the stalwart hard working 'Ds'. Though many were scrapped, a good two dozen were to outlive the 'I2s' in active service! Incidentally an official photograph was also taken in December 1907 of 'I2' class No. 11 which was the first new engine to carry the Marsh standard cast-iron chimney and have its Ramsbottom safety valves enclosed by a flared casing.

Author's Collection

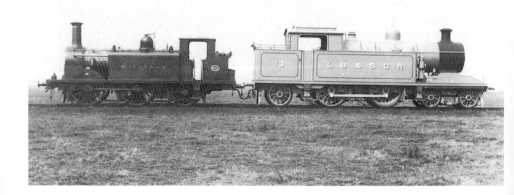

appeared between September 1908 and February 1909. Though at first designated 'I2 superheated', they became known as 'I4' since the first of the 'I3' class was already at work. In effect they emerged new from works at a time when only two 'I3s' had been constructed and were undergoing tests and further modifications before proper commencement of construction starting with No. 22 in February 1909, the same month in which the final 'I4' was completed.

Despite the knowledge of the strengths of the 'I3s' already available, performance hopes were yet again dashed, the 'I4s' being as disadvantaged as their predecessors. The problem still centred round the small firebox and grate and the unimproved front end. Despite the Schmidt superheater, they still fell short of expectations, even outshone by their kindred saturated 'I2s'. J.N. Maskelyne pinpoints their 20 in. cylinders as too large for the heating surface. The design was a flop, the small firebox offsetting the larger boiler barrel and superheater. All but one of 'I2' and 'I4' classes was withdrawn prior to World War II, No. 2034 making it to May 1940. Apart from design faults, Dr Ian C. Allen mentions another aspect of their failures. 'The operating people on the Brighton always expected these engines to do much harder work than they were up to, so the 'I1s' and 'I2s' were put onto semi-fast and outer suburban duties which they were incapable of fulfilling except under ideal conditions i.e. good preparations, good coal and a good fireman. I say this because Moorgate to Potters Bar was a cakewalk when compared with a stopper from London to Brighton or Tunbridge Wells.'

'I4' class No. 33 emerged from Brighton works in November 1908. Initially allocated to Battersea, the locomotive stands at Newhaven Harbour. The headcode denotes Victoria or Battersea Yard to Hastings via the Quarry Line, up trains from Newhaven being permitted to carry the same boards and lights as trains from Hastings to London direct. Note the splendid brass worksplates introduced by Marsh.

The 'I3' 'Wonder Engines'

In conceiving the 'I3s' Marsh had in mind main line duties on which the Billinton 'E5s' 0-6-2Ts were under-performing. By mid-1907 it was quite obvious that the 'I1s' with their 4 ft 6 in. diameter boilers would never fill that bill, so Marsh and his design team experimented by fitting five 'B4' replacement boilers together with 'B4' wheels, cylinders and motion into the frames of a 4-4-2 tank, creating in Bradley's words 'virtually a B4 with side tanks'. He expanded the 'I1' design to incorporate a 7 ft 7 in. firebox, producing a tank engine version of Billinton's 'B4' class 4-4-0s with side tanks, coal bunker and small trailing wheels in place of the tender. Marsh incorporated well-proven features, the 'B4' cylinders with slide valves below, Stephenson link motion and the Doncaster single-link type bogies which improved control and provided smoother riding. The comparatively large 6 ft 7½ in. driving wheels also added to their speediness.

But the main component responsible for the transformation was the superheater, which, it is claimed, brought Marsh lasting fame as a locomotive engineer. He had travelled extensively in Europe and was well informed on modern continental practice. By 1907 he was considering superheating. To his credit Marsh was one of the first to adopt superheating, then in its infancy, though some attribute this to B.K. Field, his chief draughtsman. Philip Evetts relates:

> Field knew that well designed steam passages plus superheating (as advised by the Schmidt Company) could produce a first class engine, which turned out exactly as he hoped. Later Marsh decided that superheating alone was the reason for the success of the 'I3', so orders were given to build the 'I4s' with superheaters, but these were no better than the 'I2s'. [He went on to elaborate:] In 1931 I went to Swindon as a Premium Apprentice, as my father was told that Brighton works was being run down for closure. John Marsh was also a pupil at Swindon and, when he heard of my origin, he said, 'I suppose you have sampled those dreadful 4-4-2 tanks that my father gave you?' I told him that the 'I3' class were wonderful engines and that I had ridden on them unofficially. He laughed and said, 'Their front ends and other features were designed by Mr Field who managed to do so when my father wasn't looking, and he should have been given the credit'. He said that the 'I1' and 'I2s' were shockers. I agreed.

The well-designed front end had much to do with the excellent performance of the 'I3s' but so also did the various improvements to the superheating arrangements. Credit must also be given to the valve setting suggested by the Schmidt Superheater Company's representative. Dr Schmidt was a friend of Marsh and came over to Brighton as his guest to set the 10 in. piston valves. However Derek Cross comments, 'I was once told Dr Schmidt never got the credit he deserved - the Brighton was a small outfit and wanted it all for themselves'. Eric Langridge bears this out in saying, 'The real kick came when Marsh got the then new Superheater Company to redesign the boiler tubing arrangement for their Schmidt superheater. The result was an astonishing economy in steam consumption per horsepower'. Through the redesign of the boiler tubing arrangement, there now appeared in March 1908 a machine comparable with the best British practice of the period. Initial results on saturated No. 21, at first fully lined out in photographic grey, were extremely successful, producing fast steady running on London expresses, Pullmans and business services, but weaknesses were apparent over the condensing gear and coal consumption, which was higher than the 'B4s' and the 'H1s'. In the light of trials with No. 22, the front-end layout was redesigned by Field in favour larger cylinders with piston valves above and an extended smokebox on a saddle. Marsh gave orders for Nos. 22-26 to be fitted with superheaters, and in May 1909 the first two were ordered from the Schmidt Superheater Co., 'fitted to 2 locomotives at £50 per locomotive'! Trials against 'B4s' and 'H1s' quickly showed the benefits of superheating in lower coal consumption, resulting in the order for a further superheated batch, Nos. 77-81. In the case of No. 22 a delay in the delivery of superheaters led Marsh to take the recently discarded boiler from 'B4' No. 47 in order to save valuable time. However, superheating involved the costs of extra equipment and royalties, which made Marsh organise comparative trials before coming off the fence. But before these trials were fully under way, the Locomotive Committee, aware of the threatening financial stringencies, insisted that a proportion of the new class should use saturated steam and this was carried out on Nos. 27-30, 75-76 which with No. 21 were later fitted with superheating between 1919 and 1927, enhanced by Field's flared safety valve casing and new Marsh chimney.

Trials with the grey-painted No. 22, fully lined out in black and white, proved the superheated 'I3' an instant success, free steaming, fast running, fit for non-stop express work by virtue of its 2,110 gallon water capacity, with decided savings in coal consumption. To boot they were both handsome and versatile and were described as 'Wonder Engines'. In performance No. 24 was the best of the early batch, being in Royal workings, but unfortunately was never the same after the Streatham Common collision of 1919, and quickly became the black sheep of the class.

The exploits of No. 23 turn and turn about with the London & North Western Railway (LNWR) on the 'Sunny South Express' in 1909 have been well featured. In that November through engine working was introduced on this train between Brighton and Rugby. No. 23 was selected, occasionally relieved by No. 26, for the round journey of 264 miles, the 90½ miles between East Croydon and Rugby were to be run non-stop without taking any water on the way. Eric Langridge writes that 'Marsh, very saucily, put the 'I3s' forward for these trials'. If so, he apparently still had some doubts and reservations for on the first few runs milk churns full of water were carried for emergency use in the front luggage compartment and 15 cwt of coal in sacks on the train. However, he need not have been worried for the condensing apparatus played its part in producing the astonishing low water consumption, together with skilfully adjusted valve settings and exemplary firing by the crew.

Spectacular results came to light when compared to the LNWR's unsuperheated 'Precursor' class 4-4-0 No. 7 *Titan*. The 'I3' won hands down in the key areas of water (22.4 against 36.6 gallons per mile) and coal consumption (27.4 against 41.2 Ib. per mile). Its timekeeping was exemplary and the economics in coal and water consumption astounded the whole locomotive world. Cecil J. Allen reckoned the coal consumption at less than 0.1 lb. per ton-mile, and J.N. Maskelyne highlighted its influence on British locomotive design generally. Langridge bluntly states that 'the LNWR tender locomotives were made to look rather silly that, no wonder, the LNWR took up Schmidt superheating straight away on Bowen Cooke's large new "George the Fifth" class 4-4-0s being built at Crewe'. Derek Cross saw the triumph in an even

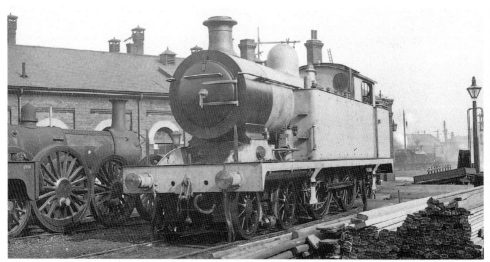

'I3' No. 22 stands outside the far corner of Brighton shed. It was the only member of the class not provided with a curved cover over the piston valves, being flat with two protrusions above the piston valve tail-rods. Because the frames were three inches shorter than the later 'I3s', it was impossible to withdraw the pistons and rods from the cylinders in the normal manner, so two holes were drilled in the buffer beam large enough to permit their passage. The seemingly antiquated locomotive on the left is in fact a set of wheels on one road and a locomotive boiler on the one beyond.   *R.C. Riley Collection*

No. 23 on the 'Sunny South Special', south of Coulsdon on the Brighton main line in 1909, possibly during the trials of that November which produced such spectacular results for the Brighton's representatives. E.T. Vyse was present to photograph this piece of history.

The LNWR's 'Precursor' No. 7 *Titan*, one of George Whales' saturated 4-4-0s, stands in Brighton station with a northbound service during the 1909 comparative trials between the two companies sharing the 'Sunny South Special' workings. The round journey from Rugby was approximately 264 miles. *Titan* is reputed to have reached Brighton on occasions with its smokebox glowing red!

'I3' No. 26 was the back-up test engine and ran to Rugby and back on just one occasion, as opposed to 11 by No. 23. Its consumption figures were only marginally inferior to those of No. 23 and streaks ahead of those turned in by *Titan*. No. 26 is seen here passing Balham Intermediate box with a down express which include Pullmans, and shows off Marsh elliptical stock to advantage. Another F. Moore photograph.

One of the later 'I3s', the superheated No. 78, heads the 'City Limited' near Coulsdon, the photograph taken by Cecil Laundy. Nos. 77 to 81 in 1910 were the last new engines to enter service bearing the full title LB&SCR on the tank sides which dates the picture to after its next visit to the shops a few years later.

A bridge weight testing exercise where the Uckfield line crossed the River Ouse just outside Lewes affords a comparison between the two early representatives of Marsh class 'I1' and a late batch 'I3'. They may look very similar but the 'I3' came up trumps on all counts. The bridge was rebuilt during 1911 and this is one of a series of photographs of the progress taken by Frank Burtt.

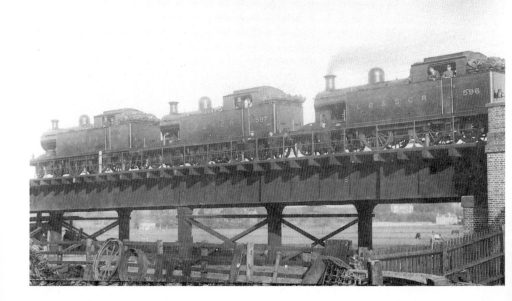

wider context, 'The Brighton gave the lordly LNWR a bloody nose!', but it was certainly these trials that forced the merits of superheating upon the reluctant attention of contemporary locomotive engineers.

Marsh had proposed to build another 10 'I3s' in 1911 but his 'indisposition' at the end of the previous December put the matter on hold. Lawson Billinton elected to complete the order and Nos. 82-91 were built between August 1912 and March 1913. Godfrey Yeomans, particularly referring to the 'I3' class, succinctly summarises the achievement:

> D.E. Marsh and B.K. Field, assisted by the Locomotive Drawing Office team, had brought the 'Brighton Locomotive' into the 20th century. A large superheated boiler, extended saddle mounted smokebox, free steam passages, piston valves and a cast-iron chimney created the Edwardian LBSC locomotive that combined business-like efficiency and functionality with an acceptable appearance that was to endure until the end of the Company's separate existence in December 1922.

With minor modifications by the Southern Railway, all but one saw out the 1939-1945 war. The bulk of the class was withdrawn in 1950-51 and No. 32091, the last to be constructed, hung on in active service, including the through Birkenhead train between Brighton and Redhill - shades of the 'Sunny South Express' to survive breaking up until 1953.

The 'J' Tanks

The Brighton, having no water troughs, always preferred the use of large tanks provided that the capacity of the water tanks was sufficient for the longer non-stop runs, and Marsh was instructed to look for locomotives of still greater power. Larger express tender engines would have caused problems at most principal running sheds, and would have called for the installation of expensive new turntables. These problems led Marsh to turn his thoughts to a powerful six-coupled tank locomotive, the six-coupled wheels proving most advantageous when accelerating away from signals and station stops.

The design was a logical development of the highly successful 'I3' class. Drawings were complete by the start of 1910 and the authorisation was given for the construction of six such locomotives at an estimated cost of £20,000. The first emerged from Brighton works near the year's end named *Abergavenny*, fitted with a Schmidt superheated parallel boiler constructed in two rings. Similar but larger in outline to the 'I3s', chimney and dome were some inches shorter to allow for the large boiler. Features included Stephenson link motion, Ramsbottom safety valves, air assisted screw reversing gear and Wakefield mechanical lubricator positioned on the left side, and a bunker coal rail to prevent spillage of fuel. Cylinders were outside and inclined as on the 'H1s', a pattern used by Lawson Billinton on his subsequent large engines. To the public they were 'massively handsome', while Bradley sums up the design as 'neat and attractive, yet suggestive of speed and power'.

Although the Brighton was one of the pioneers of high temperature superheating, the company also believed that reduced boiler pressure should go with it, and a working

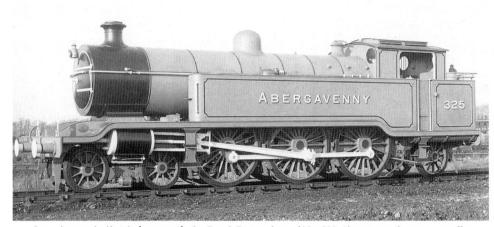

One of several official photographs by Frank Burtt taken of No. 325 *Abergavenny* but not actually on the Crumbles siding, this one showing the front end to good effect. When new in December 1910, it ran in works grey until June 1912 when standard umber was applied. The colour shown here was in fact dull grey, lined out with black bands and fine white lines, while the lettering and numerals were on white shaded with black.

Abergavenny, again in shop grey, stands at Victoria with a Brighton train via the Quarry line. Note the bogie brakes and Hasler speed recorder. The photographer is William Bennett.

pressure of 170 lb./sq. in. was selected. Teething troubles led to various alterations in February 1911, by which time Marsh was absent from the scene, and it was left to his successor to run a series of comparative trials among the leading Brighton classes. No. 325 ran indicator test trials in dull grey works livery with a degree of lining out. Results gave some concern in the area of coal consumption, unsteadiness at speed and erratic behaviour of the bogie brakes. A speed restriction of 60 mph maximum (45 mph bunker first) was imposed, water capacity was reduced from 2,300 to 2,019 gallons, (less than the economical 'I3s') improving stability and as a result the speed restrictions were lifted. Alterations were made to the blastpipe and firegrate. The modifications proved satisfactory enough to commence a second 4-6-2T in May 1911. Meanwhile in June 1912 a feedwater heater and a Weir boiler feed pump were fitted, and new test runs with both 'Js' took place that summer, listed in great detail by Bradley, but importantly showing that fuel consumption had improved.

No. 326 *Bessborough*, named after the Brighton Chairman, was virtually a slightly modified version of No. 325. As class 'J2' it was fitted with Walschaert's gear but retained the same boiler pressure. Construction began in May 1912 by which time Billinton had incorporated a number of alterations to the design. These included Walschaert's valve gear placed outside the frames, working the piston valves through rocking shafts, coiled springs in pairs below leading coupled and driving wheels, a reduction of water capacity to 1,989 gallons, a feed water heater and condensing gear. *Bessborough* carried a distinctive whistle designed by B.K. Field and entered service in umber livery.

It proved to be more successful than its sister, and Bert Perryman rated it the finest locomotive in the system, clocking 80 mph on the up 'Southern Belle' just north of Three Bridges in 1912. Overall it proved the faster of the pair with better acceleration, attributable to Walschaert's valve gear. Yet enginemen, except in adverse circumstances, found the smaller superheated 'I3s' performed equally well, and were totally convinced that the 'H2' Atlantics had the edge. Various modifications were made to both locomotives during the second Billinton regime. In 1935 further reductions were made to the height of both engines to conform with the Southern Railway's new composite loading gauge, with rounded cabs and flattened dome cover and resiting of the whistle.

Some hold that the move by Marsh to 4-6-2Ts was a vindication of Robert Billinton's 4-6-0 tender engine, plans for which were cut short owing to the designer's death. But why only one of each, for it had been Marsh's intentions to build more? Certainly they were outclassed by the 'H2' 4-4-2s, but in all probability Lawson Billinton had the yet more powerful 'L' class Baltic tanks firmly in the frame with the intention of clipping a further 10 minutes from the Victoria-Brighton schedule. Derek Cross appears to be puzzled: 'What is most interesting is that the 4-6-2T was never really taken up in Britain, despite the fact that it would seem to be ideal'. Certainly Marsh's adaptation of giant tank engines for main line working was closely watched by the South Eastern & Chatham Railway (SECR) and other companies across the country, and indeed developed to vast sizes until the Sevenoaks disaster of 1927 appeared to cast the blame on the long water tanks. Nevertheless Brighton Baltics and the Southern 'River' class were converted to tender locomotives. The more moderately sized 'Js' escaped alteration and soldiered on in secondary services until June 1951.

No. 325 seen in charge of the 'Southern Belle' set in the erstwhile rural surroundings of Norbury. After an initial running-in period on the west coast line semi-fasts and slows, it was set to work from Brighton shed on London expresses and gave an excellent account of itself.

Author's Collection

This January 1922 photograph was taken at Brighton by J.N. Maskelyne. It shows to good effect the later alterations made by Lawson Billinton, including Ross pop safety valves, Weir feed pump, condensing equipment, oval buffers and no roof cab clerestory. Bogie brakes, speed recorder and auxiliary guard irons have been removed.

An early glimpse for the photographer, W.V. Dunning, of No. 326 in works grey on a trial trip up to London. The location is the stabling point outside Victoria.

No. 326 receives its name *Bessborough* and livery of lined works grey for the official photograph at the Crumbles line ballast branch outside Eastbourne. Alterations made to the initial design by Lawson Billinton included Walschaert's valve gear, the use of spiral springs for the leading coupled and driving wheels, reduced tank capacity, addition of condensing gear and a Weir pump bolted horizontally beneath the footplate.

P.2. Boiler No. 913 Class J Maker "B.&.A.W.s" Date Built December 1910 Card No. 272
—M.I.—290.

PLATES: Barrel | Throat | Casing Covering | Casing Back | Steel Tube | Copper Wrapping | Copper Firebox | Copper Tube | Holes Bushed

STAYS: Roof Nuts Renewed | Roof Renewed | Transverse Renewed | Tube Plate Renewed | Longitudinal Renewed | Nuts Renewed | Steel Riveted over | Copper Riveted over | Steel Renewed | Copper Renewed

In or Out of Frame | Lagging Off | Steam Test | Water Test | Mileage to Date | Engine No. | Date of Entry

Record card for boiler No. 913 which spent its working life with 'J' class 4-6-2T No. 325.

Gerard Collins Collection

Bessborough on test run at Littlehampton, one of several portraits taken on this occasion in the spring of 1912 by F.W. Spry, a local photographer. In this instance the headcode discs have been changed for the return to Brighton.

No. 326 *Bessborough* stands on Brighton shed fitted with an indicator shield. Various test runs were made with the 'J' tanks in 1912. In a recorded run for No. 326 on 1st December with the 11.00 am Victoria to Brighton with seven Pullmans, a 280 ton load, 73 mph was reached at Horley. The record states: 'Weather, bright with light showers, moderate headwind. Coal good quality and size, some dust; burnt well with moderate ash and some clinkering.'

T.B. Welch/R.C. Riley Collection

The R.J. Billinton Carriage Inheritance

Marsh was not only locomotive superintendent but held the superintendence of the Carriage and Wagon Department as well and, though indirectly involved with rolling stock design, nevertheless held the responsibility for direction of the combined departments. However, as has been said, 'Marsh was much more interested in engines'. He inherited from his predecessor a stock that was largely six-wheeled and without lavatories together with a fair proportion of bogie stock, mainly in suburban 'Block' sets which compared favourably in comfort with other local trains of the period. Electric lighting had begun to come in from the start of the century using Stone's system. Hamilton Ellis was rather more disparaging: 'The Company fielded the many complaints about the scarcity of lavatories in ordinary coaches by reminding clients that Pullman cars were available for this use upon a small supplementary payment'.

L.E. Brailsford, a keen coaching enthusiast who travelled regularly in the company's trains and wrote from first hand experience, noted that Marsh confined himself almost entirely to building main line stock. 'As far as can be ascertained he never built a 4 or 6 wheeled vehicle.' Whilst retaining the Brighton trademark arrangements of panelling the exteriors of the distinctive door handles and guard rails, the 17½ in. buffers and bogie frames, in other details new ground was broken, turning out longer and much higher carriages almost up to the Brighton's generous loading gauge limit. The characteristic lookout wing to guard's compartments disappeared, the occupant having to be content with two windows at the back of his compartment. Around 1908 a change was made in bogie construction, Fox's pressed steel type being given up and steel girder sections used for the main members with horn plates being riveted on and interconnected by a cross-tie, which made for even better riding.

As with Basil Field, his chief draughtsman in regard to the design of his locomotives, it was difficult to assess the exact nature of Marsh's input with regard to carriages and wagons but, as hinted by P.J. Newbury and Hamilton Ellis, it can be stated with a fair degree of confidence that Albert Harry Panter was responsible for carriage design, Marsh stating the requirements and seeing to the administration and financial aspects. Even then one can never say that one man designed a railway's locomotives and coaches. Incidentally, Hamilton Ellis credits Panter with improvements in carriage design during the Billinton period.

Panter came from excellent antecedents, his father, W. Panter, had been carriage superintendent of the LSWR from 1885 to 1905. Albert Panter, following service at Wolverton (and it is worth noting that Brailsford observed that his new type of axlebox for the LB&SC looked an exact copy of those standard on the LNWR), moved on to the Leeds Forge Company. After two separate spells at Eastleigh, he was appointed in 1888 as general foreman of the LB&SC Carriage Department. In 1904 this title was amended to manager of the Carriage and Wagon Construction Branch of the Locomotive and Carriage Department. Following Marsh's departure the cumbersome department was separated and Panter became carriage and wagon superintendent in his own right, installed at the new purpose-built works at Lancing. Though a Board Minute of 13th July, 1904 discussed land purchase for a future Lancing works, and its intent was confirmed on 13th October, 1905, the scheme in total was not approved until 1907. Construction was under way in 1909, and it is likely that a certain amount of carriage work was undertaken there in Marsh's last year in office.

From 1905 onwards Panter introduced a new standard length vehicle of 54 ft and a maximum width of 8 ft 6 in. for main line stock across a whole variety of types. Yet, apart from central passageways in some of the prestige stock, P.J. Newbury comments, 'It is surprising, considering contemporary practice, that the LB&SCR should not have built any corridor stock'. A vestibuled corridor train had been authorized in 1898 but nothing came of it despite the Brighton's neighbours to the north and west showing the way. With corridors came access to lavatory accommodation, and criticism was fairly pronounced since this facility was being made available on first class accommodation on other railways. Perhaps the Brighton considered that just over an hour non-stop in a few extreme cases was outweighed by the 99 per cent who used semi-fasts and all station stoppers, and where well nigh every station on the system had toilet facilities at hand. Jonathan Abson suggests the reason was partly economics, a corridor lavatory coach seating only 36 compared with an ordinary compartment coach accommodating 56, and this is borne out in a Board Minute of 18th October, 1905 when Marsh's suggestion of a corridor train was turned down 'as they would afford less accommodation'.

Elliptical Stock

Today the term 'Balloon' has become largely confined to the copious 8 ft 10 in. trailer cars used on the motor services and the term 'elliptical' to the several sets of main line stock in various combinations built from 1905 onwards. They were so named because of their outstanding features, the high roof whose top stood just under 13 ft above rail level, impressive when compared to the previously standard arc roof. The roof is best technically described as a 'barrel roof, made up of various curves, neither being truly semi-circular or elliptical, but rather blending both'. There were several different types of elliptical stock, all being produced in small quantities, the result of several compromises to meet conflicting requirements handed down from above.

Urgent for the image of the line was the need to provide special new carriages for the stockbrokers' all first class non-stop express up from Brighton to London Bridge at 8.45 am, returning at 5 pm which came to be known as the 'City Limited'. Albert Panter therefore set out to design a set of carriages that were never to be surpassed during the remainder of the company's existence, and very comfortable and airy coaches they were too. On the up journey with the new stock a two- or three-coach portion plus a Pullman were slipped at East Croydon. The new carriages went into service in the summer of 1907 having been inspected by the Directors at London Bridge following the Board Meeting of 13th March. The bodies of the slipped section, 9 ft wide at their waist and 8 ft 6 in. at cantrail, gave the impression of being blown out. The set comprised a mix of coaches, some interconnected with vestibules, others semi-corridors together with luxury saloons, all of varying lengths.

Elliptical stock bogie composite No. 523 was the second of four to be built at Brighton in December 1906. The first class compartments, which seated three a side, were placed in the centre with two second class compartments, each seating five a side, at the ends. One first and two second class compartments were labelled 'Smoking'. No lavatories were included.

Marsh elliptical-roofed boat train set No. 87, complete with roof destination boards. Built in 1907, it included two second class brakes, a third brake and the unique full brake No. 191 nearest the camera. The several brakes were needed for the London Bridge portion, besides conveying large quantities of luggage. The boat train waits in the road adjacent to the platform at Newhaven Marine with a Marsh Atlantic tank at its head.

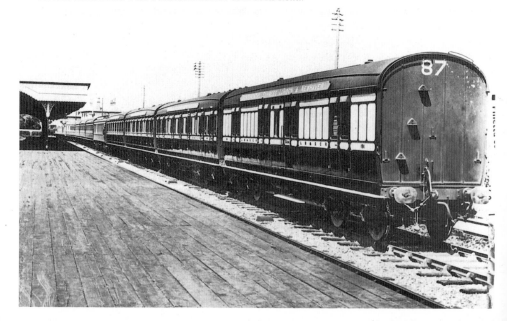

Hamilton Ellis describes the superb formation:

The first three coaches had vestibule entrance instead of the usual side doors. At one end was a 54ft saloon-brake with lighting dynamo and end lavatory, followed by a parlour saloon and a unique side corridor coach, the former, with two saloons internally subdivided with a central lavatory, the latter with six 'roomy' compartments and two lavatories. The saloon compartments were furnished with a limited number of fixed seats of superior first class type, and with upholstered bucket chairs . . . [next came the Pullman Cars] . . . Further carriages were more like the new standard stock including Lavatory Firsts and a First Brake, but with the doors recessed to allow for the 9 ft width at waist. [For a fuller description see Newbury, page 60.]

The coach bogies incorporated a new type of axlebox and two stanchions took the truss bar strain instead of Billinton's central one, and the bar had midway an adjustable shackle. All the main line vehicles were electrically lit on Stone's system.

Several sets of the elliptical stock were built, one being on the 'Crowborough Express' complete with roof boards, in 1907-8, while some special designs for the Boat train to Newhaven were made 56 ft long, fitted with 4-wheel bogies having a wheelbase of 10 ft averaging a weight of 27 tons. Deep ornamental brass electroliers were fitted to house electric lights, but sadly the set was not fitted with corridors or vestibules. The new Continental Boat Train boasted one unique vehicle, a bogie brake van with central guard's compartment. The stock when new rode very comfortably, but critics noted that the ellipticals later did not ride well, presumably through being top heavy. On 1st November, 1908, the new 'Southern Belle' Pullman train was introduced to supersede 'The Pullman Ltd', but these cars were in the British Pullman Car Company ownership and did not come directly under Marsh's aegis.

Regarding the rail motor 'Balloon' trailers briefly mentioned on pages 23-25 each had a capacity of 52 passengers in separate smoking and non-smoking saloons, seated in the contemporary American tramcar style with reversible seats rattan, and with a control trailer compartment at the end. The inside headroom was 8 ft 7¾ in. with a deep elliptical roof, 12 ft 11 in. rail to rooftop and this gained them the nickname 'Balloon' coaches. Passengers entered through end doors and vestibules. Later some of the Panter high-roofed carriages were used to provide additional accommodation on the expanding auto services, previously mentioned, to supplement the original third class 'Balloon' trailers built from 1905 through to the Great War. Later still additionally large numbers of auto-trailers of the more usual compartment type were built, many in 2-car formations.

David Gould notes that for some reason, following the introduction of several sets of elliptical roofed carriages, the LB&SCR appeared to have second thoughts and reverted to its former standards of carriage construction with an arc of 7 ft radius, 11 ft 9½ in. in height above rail level, and suggests that 'the reason for the regression was that the "Balloon" coaches had restricted route availability'. Another factor may well have been the already mentioned turn of the financial tide through overstretch resulting from the rapid expansion in locomotive and rolling stock construction during the first half of Marsh's regime, the push for electric train sets and the implementation of the

Newly-formed elliptical Set No. 50 on its maiden run pauses at Lewes behind 'D3' class 0-4-4T No. 374. The leading coach is bogie lavatory third brake No. 719 which in December 1915 was taken into ambulance train No. 25, and was never returned to passenger service though the underframes were re-used for new arc-roofed coach bodies in 1922.

One of the two elliptical-roof trailer third brakes to diagram 179, known as 'Balloons' on account of their roof profile, photographed under construction at Brighton in 1905.

John Minnis Collection

Driving trailer composite brake No. 633 was rebuilt at Lancing in 1909 from a six- wheeled third to provide some first class accommodation which the 'Balloon' trailers did not have. Use was made of former six-wheel five-compartment third bodies mounted on new 54 ft underframes with two additional compartments plus a driver's compartment at one end. The early members of the batch were among the last to receive the umber and white livery.

Bogie third brake No. 467 of 1908 was one of Marsh's most numerous type of rebuilds. On a new bogie underframe was placed a 30 ft third body and a shortened and modified six-wheel guard's van body which had two sets of double doors on each bodyside. It incorporated five compartments plus guard's van with centrally placed duckets. An O.J. Morris photograph taken at New Cross in the early 1920s.

electrification scheme, the rolling programme of station rebuilding, especially at Victoria, the line widening, together with the reconstruction of Brighton works, immediately followed by the new carriage works at Lancing.

From 1907 onwards the company built very few new carriages for steam working. The Board, on 20th March, 1907, decided that the construction of carriage and wagon stock on renewal and capital account be discontinued. In future new stock was to be obtained by contract work with only repairs carried out in the company's shops, until such times Lancing came on line. The LB&SCR now resorted to buying a very large number of 6-wheeled carriages into bogie stock on the new standard 54 ft underframes, which allowed for the withdrawal of the greater part of the older Stroudley stock. However, the converted stock was to be lit with incandescent gas, less expensive than electricity. The rebuilds came in a whole range of combinations in all three classes, of lavatory brake composites and even tri-composites, the great majority being formed into standard 3-coach sets, each formed of a third brake, a composite and another third brake, with ample loose 'spares' to strengthen normal trains or create makeshift formations as required. At the end of Marsh's regime came the abolition of second class accommodation, in the suburban area in June 1911 and on the main line services a year later, the exception being the Newhaven Boat Train, which, because of an agreement with the Brighton's French counterparts, retained all three classes until 1925.

Electrification

When it came to the implementing the Company's Act of 1903 giving it powers to electrify part of its system, Marsh had a more prominent role, particularly on the technical side. The stock was designed jointly by Marsh and Philip Dawson, the car bodies' specification settled by Dawson with the approval of the Locomotive Department who were responsible for the contract of electrical equipment, and ordered for the South London line from the Metropolitan Amalgamated Railway Carriage & Wagon Company of Saltley (Birmingham). They were quite unlike any previous LB&SC carriages in their style featuring squared-body moulding, hinged opening top lights and roof coverings of aluminum. Along each 60 ft car the open side corridor changed sides at mid-point. The 3-coach sets lacked gangways between cars and any heating, but were much more generously dimensioned and luxurious than contemporary suburban stock elsewhere. Later, trailer composites were built at the new Lancing works in the LB&SCR's more usual style. A maintenance depot was established at Peckham Rye where the substation supplied electric power at 6,700 volts AC. The electrical and mechanical equipment was the particular design of Dawson. The electric sets are described in considerable detail by Hamilton Ellis. Regarding the cost of electrification, Pelham Maitland maintained that none of the electric rolling stock was provided from new capital but covered from the Repairs and Renewals Fund, in Ellis' words, [a] 'triumph of actuarial ingenuity'.

The success of the new electric trains was undisputed, and in July 1910 the Crystal Palace group of lines were next slated for conversion. However the limitations of the old Crystal Palace (Low Level) and Leigham tunnels meant that this order for stock had to be built to conform to the lesser dimensions of the Brighton steam stock. Compartments were full width without side corridors, a driver's compartment in each vehicle ensuring maximum flexibility of operation. Despite being equipped with more powerful traction motors, there was a significant reduction in weight, as indeed in the overhead gantries, and the carriages were all long-buffered in line with main line stock. The usual formation consisted of a motor third with luggage compartment and cab, running between two composite central trailers, a pair making up a peak-hour 6-coach train. Services from Victoria to Crystal Palace commenced on the 12th May, 1911, but Marsh had left the scene by the time the full service was running over the whole group of lines via Streatham Hill and Tulse Hill. An electric car shed was established at Selhurst.

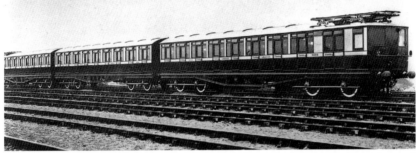

Comparative views of the two types of early electric stock. *Above:* a newly outshopped South London line three-coach set, comprising motor coach No. 3203, first class trailer and a third class trailer converted from steam stock, proudly displays its two-tone livery. Within a year the accommodation provided by the stock was found to be over-lavish, and in 1910-11 the first class trailer was taken out and transferred to steam use, while the motor coaches were reformed with new trailers. The lower picture shows a complete 'Crystal Palace' six-car train with motor third brake at its head. Constructed by the Metropolitan Amalgamated Railway Carriage & Wagon Co. of Birmingham, David Gould suggests the new stock was posed at Saltley where it is carrying a headcode never actually used by the LB&SCR.

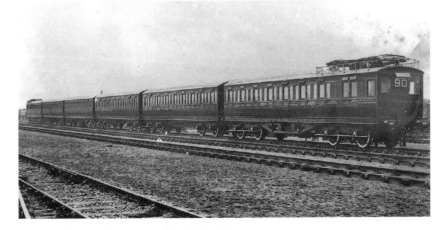

The sole 'B3' class 4-4-0, No. 213 *Bessemer*, powers the Continental boat train past Wandsworth Common. At the front of the train is one of the 'Grand Vitesse' vans.

H.C.F. Small/Bluebell Archives

Carriage No. 4074 was a driving trailer composite built at Lancing in 1913 for the Crystal Palace electric services, having three first and five third class compartments. Note the electric conduits on the roof to each compartment to light the carriage. The livery of the 'CP' stock was all-over brown from the start, with yellow and black lining. Taken by O.J. Morris at Crystal Palace.

20 ton triple bolster wagon No. 7281, shown as outshopped in November 1909. The 1910 LB&SCR diagram for these wagons states that the vehicles could not negotiate curves of less than 5 chains radius. This one was rebuilt with many modifications as a four-wheeled aeroplane truck at Lancing early in 1917.

Passenger Vans and Goods Stock

One notable development while Marsh was in charge was the construction of several vans, classified as non-passenger coaching stock but fitted and sprung to run in passenger trains, for various traffics between 1906 and 1910. On 17th March, 1905 the Brighton's Officers Conference of leading departmental heads pointed to the need for additional vehicles for conveyance of 'Grand Vitesse' traffic. Of interest was the stipulation that the locomotive superintendent, when proposing new stock, should also furnish a list of vehicles proposed for their breaking up during the same period, thus tying the new to the redundant as rolling stock renewals. Marsh was also asked to arrange hire of some 20 ton trucks for trial that might be introduced with advantage. The first design was for the 'Grande Vitesse' continental perishables traffic, suitably marked in gold italics, and for the West Sussex coast fruit traffic. They were 30 ft long and carried 4½ tons, with ventilation slats fitted down both sides and at the ends. There followed a similar design with slats in the doors only. Nominally classified for luggage, they were both specialist and multifarious in their scope, being used for different categories of traffic such as fruit, fish and milk. Six butter vans appeared in 1910 incorporating a double roof for insulation. Two experimental horseboxes had been constructed in 1907 featuring two boxes per vehicle. All these designs conveniently used the underframes from the rebuilt Billinton 6-wheel passenger stock.

Availability of these underframes led to some experimental vehicles designed by Panter namely a unique bogie refrigerator van of 1905 using a 38 ft length, which did not correspond to any of the existing carriage underframes. The 1908-10 periods saw the construction of a 6-wheeled ballast wagon and a 6-wheeled triple bolster wagon. Regretfully they were not perpetuated, the company preferring its tried and trusted small vehicles, a retrograde step as with the carriages. As a result the wagon stock development failed to keep pace with changing needs and fell behind, comparing unfavourably with the best that could be had on the neighbouring LSWR and SECR. The standards set by Stroudley remained almost unaltered in bodywork, only improving in the quality of the more modern brakes and running gear. The wagon stock Marsh inherited was not only very close to the maximum number the company had at any time, but a goodly proportion of it was newly-built, leaving Marsh with really very little to do. Although well maintained, even in Marsh's time, the goods fleet presented a very uniform and dated appearance. This retarded development was to lead the Southern Railway to pass over its Brighton inheritance and in this field adopt the policies and standards of its two other constituents.

Hamilton Ellis dismisses the Brighton wagon stock saying that, apart from the distinctly superior van stock the fleet 'was no better than on most British railways, which is not saying much!' The only designs really new to the Brighton was the 12 ton mineral wagons bought from Hurst Nelson, and also their outstanding 20 ton steel ballast hopper wagon, the latter initiated by Robert Billinton before his death. Other than the above, Marsh seems to have contented himself with building the largest capacity versions of existing designs when replacements were called for. The major traffic in coal was mostly carried in from northern firms, the LB&SCR possessing relatively few mineral wagons, chiefly to offload the coal at Deptford, Littlehampton and Shoreham, whilst their locomotive coal was contracted out to Messrs Stephenson Clarke & Co.

Panter was left a free hand in carriage and wagon construction subject to Board approval and financial costing, and in the middle Marsh period was totally absorbed in the organization of the new carriage and wagon works at Lancing, successfully brought into production in April 1909. This removed him one step further away from Marsh and two years later, with the latter's resignation, the Locomotive and Carriage Departments were separated, Albert Panter becoming carriage and wagon superintendent in his own right.

Liveries

In 1903 Robert Billinton had made a change in the colour scheme of the Brighton's main line stock, introducing umber on the lower quarter and mouldings with white upper panels, which were slightly creamy under varnish. Marsh, at the Directors' request in the search for a less expensive yet workmanlike livery, was asked not only to look at the locomotives but also at the carriage finish. Marsh organised an exhibition of new and newly-painted stock at Brighton in 1905, specimen coaches being finished in the old mahogany, in green and in green and cream. The style adopted was umber, the paint technically labelled 'purple brown', akin to but less purple than that of the LNWR. Panels were painted white, but the suburban sets were umber all over apart from the electrics, which received the two-tone livery. Unfortunately this attractive livery was short-lived, and from 1910 the white panels were dropped and all the steam stock was repainted in umber, lined out in yellow and black, the Royal Train and the odd saloon being the only exceptions.

A new goods livery was introduced near the end of Marsh's time early in 1911, with lead grey for the bodywork and solebars in a shade believed to have been darker than in the Billinton period. Van roofs were painted white. The non-passenger coaching stock was painted umber with white roofs.

Summary

David Gould in his appraisal concludes that 'Carriage stock was not perhaps the LB&SCR's strongest point'. Most of the company's carriage stock was basically suburban with self-contained compartments and scarcity of lavatory accommodation. It had fallen well behind the larger neighbours, persisting with its old-fashioned plain arc roofs, and widespread electrification of the Southern Railway's Central section provided a ready excuse to dispose of the majority. Marsh's term of office had started with many new ideas and improvements but, under the financial restraint that set in during the middle of his reign, the impetus of true modernisation fell back and never caught up again across the years leading to the Grouping. The stringency during the Great War, which broke out only three years after Marsh's resignation, put paid to any new large scale developments.

Chapter Three

Improvements

Rebuilding Brighton Works

When Marsh arrived at Brighton there were other pressing needs, not so much creating something that was new as improving what was already there. The chief of these was a growing backlog of repairs, the reconstruction of the Brighton works and the search for a new and less expensive livery at the time that the company had overstretched its resources and was under severe financial restraint. Marsh realised that it was distinctly cheaper to improve the performance of current locomotives, underpowered in coping with increasing loads demanded, than to construct new ones. The Brighton, moreover, had a long history of extended contracts with outside manufacturers, most notably in the locomotive department. Having the work done in house would prove more cost effective.

In order to achieve these objectives, the key lay in the modernisation of the company's principal works at Brighton. Towards the end of Robert Billinton's term of office, Brighton was finding it difficult to maintain the locomotive stock in good mechanical order. It was becoming increasingly impossible to pass through the works the large number of locomotives needing attention. Consequently members of all classes were having to spend many months, sometimes years, laid aside in store, awaiting vacant berths in shops. Roads Nos. 6, 7 and 8 in Brighton Loco yard were full of these invalids at this time. Minor improvements and rearrangements had hardly scratched the surface. The bulk of the 'B4' 'Scotchmen' had been ordered from Sharp, Stewart & Co. in order to ease pressure, and the matter had been exacerbated by a full building programmed for the 'E5' and 'E6' 0-6-2Ts urgently needed in the London area. As a result 'heavy' repairs to the existing stock began to accumulate.

Although Robert Billinton had begun to extend the works by building out and over the goods roads which occupied the eastern end of the cliff on which works were sited, even these had been quickly surpassed by the demands of repair and new construction, and it fell to the new incumbent to bring about a solution. The works were so miserably cramped that there was, for instance, no direct rail connection between the carriage underframe erecting shop and the body shop, although the buildings were adjacent. All completed underframes had to be passed out of the works at the London end, run round, and passed in at the Brighton end for the bodies to be fitted.

To circumvent this Marsh had initially proposed constructing a line in from the Lewes and Hastings line into Brighton works which would require a bridge over New England Road. The portion proposed to be covered in for use as an extension of the storage accommodation was pointed out by Marsh at the meeting of Engine Stock Committee at Brighton on Friday 13th October, 1905. 'The proposal is to build a bridge from the rail level of the buildings on one side of the road slopes to the rail level of the buildings on the other side, and to cover the whole road space laterally

The tight constraints of the carriage shop at Brighton with rolling stock under repair taking nearly all the available space. By this time Marsh had moved the wagon underframes to a separate shop. An American-built Pullman receives attention on the right. Billinton bogie stock is under construction while an inverted six-wheel underframe is visible in the centre. The transfer of the Carriage & Wagon Department to Lancing released much space for the expansion of the Locomotive Works. A W.G. Tilling photograph.   *John Minnis Collection*

The spacious avenues of Lancing works contrast with the restricted confines of the Brighton carriage shop it superseded. A variety of Marsh period stock in the 'interim' carriage livery is on view. Construction had proceeded slowly during Marsh's time and, though some carriage and wagon work began from 1907, *The Railway News* for 29th March, 1913 confirmed that the works had only been brought into full use during the previous 12 months.

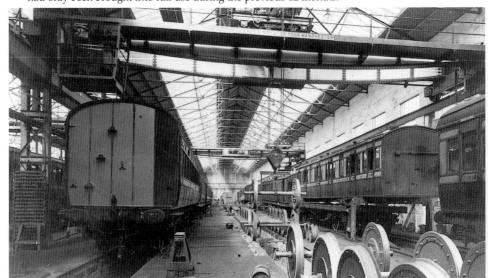

from one bridge now crossing it to the other. The area thus obtained would be approximately ¾ of an acre, the cost roughly estimated at £25,000.'

Marsh next produced plans of the shops and how he proposed they should be altered. If the New England Road covering scheme was carried out, it would be necessary to rebuild and enlarge the present erecting shop and absorb a building used by the Stores Department. If the wagon repair shop were to go to Lancing, its area of 3¾ acres would provide a more advantageous arrangement and give greater opportunity for future expansion than adopting the New England Road scheme.

The Committee proposed the following recommendations:

1. The bridge scheme for England Road be abandoned.
2. The whole of the Carriage and Wagon Works and Wagon Repair Shops be removed as soon as possible from Brighton. (This principle was adopted by the Directors on 18th October ordering plans to be prepared by the Engineer for the new shops at Lancing in consultation with the locomotive superintendent.)
3. The present Carriage Shop be converted into a locomotive erecting shop with the necessary yard.
4. The shop to be connected by bridge or subway with the present shops on the down side, and the Engineer to report on the advantages of the two plans as soon as possible.
5. The present wagon repairing shop be converted into a 'stable' for engines.
   It concluded: No further delay should take place in the removal of the Carriage & Wagon Department from Brighton.

The fact was that when Marsh had to make further extensions there was only one course open to him, the Carriage Department had to be removed to a new site, at Lancing.

The Board, fully aware of these problems, outlined their proposals at the meeting on the 11th July, 1906, namely a carriage and wagon works at Lancing and a remodelling of Brighton locomotive works. The plan for Lancing, after modifications, was approved at a cost of £185,190 on 20th February, 1907, later reduced by £60,000 on the 17th April, the improvements to the shops at Brighton costing £84,359. But on the 3rd July as a result of a diminution in the company's receipts for the first half of the year, it was decided only to proceed with those parts of Brighton and Lancing works authorised and 'absolutely necessary'. Marsh was instructed in consultation with the General Manager to explore the possibility of effecting a reduction of £12,500 in renewal of stock expenditure and a similar reduction in the following half-year, and submit a report on how he proposed to achieve this.

This was all part of the company's larger financial problem that became so acute in 1907. The company's finances were in a parlous position at this point through having too many capital projects running concurrently, being listed in a Minute of 6th November, 1907. In addition to the immense outlay involved in rebuilding Brighton works and building from new at Lancing, there were installation costs of the South London Line electrification, the enlargement of Victoria station, improvements at Worthing and Seaford stations, line widening at Battersea, Clapham Junction (involving a new station and diversion of the West London Extension Railway), on the main line from Earlswood to Three Bridges and between Sutton

A glimpse during the works reconstruction of the builder's yard with heaps of gravel, stacks of timber and planks and scaffolding poles, the latter visible on the right propped up against the wall of a building that was later to receive an additional storey. The framework for the new shops can be seen in the left background. *Gerard Collins Collection*

Another view of the enlargement upwards for the new erecting shop in 1908. It was this state of affairs that made Marsh lay off several hundred men during the winter which caused hardship and unrest amongst the workforce. There is much of interest to be seen and an unusual vista through the demolished side wall.

and Cheam, and a new engine shed at Eastbourne. 'The Company will require a loan of £800,000 from the bankers before payment of the February dividend.'

Reductions were made in the cost of rebuilding Victoria station and the renewal of Crowborough tunnel. Marsh's cost cutting came through his submission to build only five instead of 10 authorised locomotives (these refer most probably to the second series of 'I1' tanks where only the first 10 of the order of 20 were eventually built). This produced a saving of £11,500, and in any case could not have been constructed due to the current upheaval and restricted shop space at Brighton works. For the following half-year he proposed that five of the new engines be charged to the renewal account. In the interim Marsh undertook some internal reorganisation, carriage and wagon underframes being built in separate shops pending the completion of the new rolling stock works. When the latter became ready, the wagon shop at Brighton was handed over to the Locomotive Department for running repairs.

A similar state of affairs existed in the erecting shop where delays were the result of poor organisation. Some of the problems could partially be overcome by the introduction of more spare boilers; the only way out of the impasse was both a reorganisation and improvement to the overall facility at Brighton works. Marsh persuaded the Directors to allocate some £60,000 to modernise the boiler (£41,850) and smith's shops (£17,700), work carried out between May 1906 and March 1907 with the aim of obviating in the future the need to subcontract the building of new locomotives to private manufacturers.

But in the interim with a number of shops closed for reconstruction, the whole situation was made doubly worse. Marsh had no option but to follow the course already set out by his predecessor, namely to store locomotives waiting for major overhaul that could not be undertaken at Brighton and New Cross, at places other than in the works yards, and to place orders for locomotives or parts with outside builders. So Marsh contracted his first five Atlantics with Kitsons, ordered five copper fireboxes from the Yorkshire Engine Co. Ltd, some new boilers from the North British Railway and sent some wagons for repairs to Willesden and New England. The increasing outside costs involved so alarmed the Brighton Directors that they hauled him over the coals for trying to keep abreast of new construction and routine overhauls in using private manufacturers to solve the problem! In 1907 he had contracted with the Yorkshire Engine Company to repair 10 'E4s', which were dispatched via the LB&SC and Midland routes, running on their own wheels. This led to censure and the call for a thorough enquiry by an independent locomotive engineer into the efficiency of Brighton works.

Robert Urie of the LSWR was engaged and reported back in July 1908. The Brighton company's poor showing stunned the Locomotive Committee who insisted on the reduction of repairs and construction costs, but refused to authorise the recruitment of more skilled men to avoid the cost of overtime and weekend working. Nor did they take account that Battersea, New Cross and Brighton running sheds had repaired a total of 74 engines and 43 tenders, in many cases heavy or general repairs. At peak periods new ex-works engines were sent out into traffic without being repainted. The fact was that Brighton works had neither the facilities nor manpower to keep abreast of current repair commitments at the time.

During the crisis caused by the reorganisation of Brighton works which caused a vast backlog of locomotives awaiting repair and a resultant shortage in the stock of working engines, 'E4' No. 512 was amongst several pressed straight from overhaul into service as yet unrepainted and running in lead undercoat. The location is Hove station in August 1908, and the photographer is William Bennett.   *M.P. Bennett/Bluebell Archives*

The roof over the wheel shop was raised by 13 ft, and the framework is placed in position. In the foreground is the open area occupied by the wheel store. Hundreds of wheel sets all painstakingly and precisely stacked, which have been brought in from outside foundries, await their turn as part of an extensive wagon construction programme. In the background locomotive wheels await turning.

Against this very trying backcloth Marsh progressed the reconstruction as swiftly as possible, at the same time beginning to extend the system of stocking spare boilers. Replacing a worn or damaged boiler with an identical one drawn from stores allowed an engine to go into service again without delay. This scheme had been hinted at by Robert Billinton but Marsh claimed the credit for its general introduction as he extended it to cover practically every class of engine. Marsh found it necessary to enlarge the wheel shop, overlooking the former wheel yard at the seaward end of the main building. To achieve this it was necessary to extend upwards - the only option - by lifting bodily by 13 ft the old roof over the wheel and Westinghouse shops, and then adding brick courses to the existing walls until they had risen high enough to meet it. However, the centre portion, which contained Chester Craven's office, was left intact. All the new shops had to be supported on masonry pillars, and the old entrance in New England Road had to be diverted and later closed altogether.

On 18th March, 1908 the Board approved the introduction of electric power for Brighton works and the cost of equipping the machinery for electrical working was granted on 1st July. Later that year, the works was connected to the Brighton electricity supply, all the machinery was converted to electric drive and the steam driven generating plant scrapped. On the other hand a steam heating plant was installed in the paint shop in the same year.

But while the works was under reconstruction, it had been necessary to store locomotives awaiting overhaul in quiet secluded parts of the system like Horsted Keynes and the as yet unopened Ashurst Spur, and delay scrapping. However the greatest disturbance, as will be seen later, was due to a great part of the workforce having to be laid off. Once into 1908 the improvements at Brighton works began to have their effect, and Marsh never again found it necessary to go to outside firms to purchase new locomotives. But the severe pressure continued awhile on the repair resources at Brighton, not alleviated by Marsh's desire to see his new 'revolutionary' locomotives on the rails at the earliest opportunity.

On 2nd October, 1910 the alterations to Brighton locomotive works were reported complete but there had been an overspend of almost £5,453 beyond authorised expenditure which was charged to the Suspense Account when Marsh left. But he was able to hand over to his successor a modernised and enlarged plant whose main block was over 600 ft long and nearly 450 ft wide at the maximum, tapering at both ends, restricted by New England Road at the north or 'country' end and by Brighton station and the Lower Goods Yard to the south and east. The principal shops included the boiler shop 505 ft long and for about half the length 126 ft wide, the erecting shop 593 ft long and 98 ft wide and the machine shop 207 ft long and 140 ft wide. Alongside the erecting shop and extending 334 ft was the forge, 54 ft wide and opening up into the smithy with the frame and wheel shops adjoining. The works also included separate iron and brass foundries, a saw mill, fitting shop, electrical shop, tool room and shops for carpenters, welders, platers, coppersmiths, millwrights and one for the Westinghouse pump equipment. In this up to date condition it was able in the coming World War to contribute to munitions production and other wartime engineering requirements.

Brighton works in the throes of reconstruction. The steel roof for the erecting shop takes shape in 1908, high above the walls of the existing buildings dating from the 1840s. Note the series of ladders reaching up into the framework, calling for the skills of a steeplejack! Lines of open 'A's stand in the yard below.

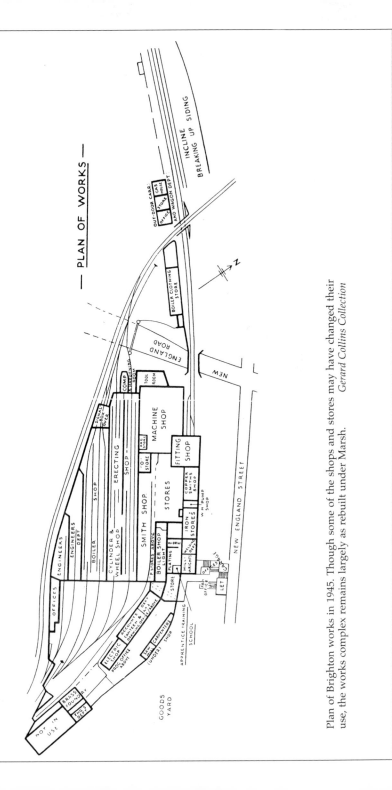

— PLAN OF WORKS —

Plan of Brighton works in 1945. Though some of the shops and stores may have changed their use, the works complex remains largely as rebuilt under Marsh.   *Gerard Collins Collection*

'E4' class No. 580 running as a 2-4-2T hurtles past Dyke Junction box with a truly amazing mix of rolling stock which looks as if it originated from Lancing works, a few miles further west. Painted in umber, the 'E4' ran converted from 1906-9.

An extremely fine portrait by William Bennett of 'E5' No. 591 *Tillington*. This locomotive was doubly noteworthy, working the 'Grand Vitesse' van trains between London Bridge and Newhaven on a regular basis; *Tillington* was also the last engine of the company to work in Stroudley livery, only losing its gamboge in 1917.

Adaptations

Marsh was a man not averse to experimentation amongst the locomotive fleet if some improvement in performance or some financial gain could be achieved. It was always worth a try even if eventually no benefit accrued and a return was made to the status quo. He was, however, a man who made up his mind speedily and quickly jumped to conclusions, but to his credit he had the courage of his convictions.

Marsh took with him from Doncaster an intense dislike of front-coupled tank engines of which the Brighton had approximately 400 out of a total of some 500 locomotives. He carried in his mind the enquiry following the Doublebois express derailment during his time at Swindon. He had noted the occasion in 1908 when a new Drummond 'M7' 0-4-4T had come off the rails at Tavistock and, nearer home, when one of the Ivatt's 0-8-2Ts had proved overweight when used on the Metropolitan Widened Lines, and required reboilering with a smaller example, plus shortening the tanks and reducing the water capacity.

Whatever his thinking, shortly after taking office at Brighton he altered 20 of Billinton's relatively new 'E5' 0-6-2 tank engines together with a pair of 'E4s' Nos. 580 and 581, to 2-4-2 wheel arrangement by removing their front coupling rod sections. J.N. Maskelyne recalls that D.E. Marsh was contemplating the construction of some 2-4-2-tank engines and used the 'E5' conversions as guinea pigs. But why convert so many? W. E. Briggs who was employed at Brighton works at the time recalled: 'The bare and sharp knuckle end left on the retained portion took the back off many fingers at running sheds'. When challenged about time lost behind these adapted 'E5s', Marsh apparently responded: 'Heavy front-coupled tank locomotives severely strained the permanent way and were not considered entirely safe at high speed; he preferred four-coupled-wheel engines for such tasks even if time was occasionally lost in bad weather'. With such justification he saw to it that his own first series of passenger tank engines were of the Atlantic wheel arrangement based on the GNR 'C12' class 4-4-2 tanks using the original Doncaster drawings. Nevertheless faced by numerous complaints and heavy hints as shed foremen put these converts onto goods rosters, all these engines were quietly reconverted to 0-6-2Ts by September 1909. Marsh had noted the complete freedom from derailment of the majority of the 0-6-2 radial tanks and, if not completely reconciled to front-coupled tank engines, at least accepted the status quo. Perhaps he had noted in passing that even his former chief, H.A. Ivatt, was building 'N1' class 0-6-2 tanks at Doncaster!

Again, barely three months in office, Marsh decided, when 0-6-0T No. 82 *Boxhill* entered works at the end of March 1905 for fitting for motor train operation by means of a rod-operated gear passing under the rear buffer beam, to convert the 'Terrier' to a 2-4-0T. No. 82 was ready in mid-July and No. 81 was similarly transformed in September 1905. These were trial conversions and after some problems with the location and efficiency of the sandboxes, the 'Terriers' completely outdid the steam and petrol cars in trials, with no failures in traffic whatever. It seems the intention was to reduce the power of the locomotives to suit the new duties, for cylinders were sleeved down 4 inches and boiler

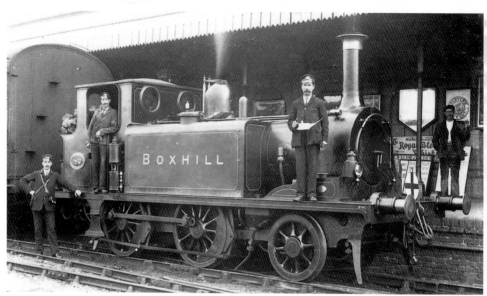

This portrait at Kemp Town shows Stroudley 'Terrier' No. 81, one of a pair selected by Marsh for conversion to a 2-4-0T, an experiment seeking to match the locomotive's power to the requirement of hauling a single 'Balloon' coach. Marsh lowered this to the extent that the pair were underpowered for graded lines and could only comfortably operate on the flat west coast line rail motors.

Stroudley's 'Gladstone' class No. 189 *Edward Blount*, a Gold medallist at the Paris Exhibition of 1889, was selected by Marsh for his experiment with Hammond's air heating apparatus in 1907, being fitted with a completely new smokebox. This ungainly gadget did not stand the test of time; within a year the apparatus was disconnected but not removed, and went for scrap with the engine when withdrawn in December 1912. This portrait was taken at one of William Bennett's favourite locations at the east end of the down platform at Hove, capturing up trains in the best light.

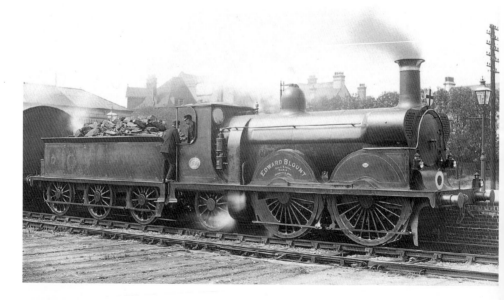

pressure reduced by 20 lb./sq. in. Marsh came to realise this had been overdone and on the second conversion No. 81 had pressure returned to 150 lb./sq. in. and cylinders back to 12 inches together with the feed water condensing pipes, removed in Billinton's time, restored in order to reduce fuel consumption. Alternative liveries, No. 81 painted umber with LB&SCR on the tank sides, No. 82 Stroudley goods green and named, were introduced to sound out public reaction.

Handel Kardas comments that 'the trouble Marsh took shows that he did not view this as a distraction from more important developments elsewhere, but it is interesting to note that the experience showed him that he could not improve much on Stroudley's original concept'. Though worth exploring, the conversion failed to signal any real benefit, in fact it limited the ability of the locomotives to cover other normal 'Terrier' duties. Both were converted back to 0-6-0Ts in 1913. However they had more than proved their point on the rail motors and in the next five years to 1909 another 20 'Terriers' were adapted for push-pull working.

Experimentation

Marsh was an experimenter at heart, as already seen in his keen interest in petrol cars and electrification, and this was no less the case with regard to his search for improvements in the steam locomotive field. He arrived at Brighton just too late to feature in the brief period when various Brighton engines were equipped for oil burning in 1902-03, the merits of which had been demonstrated by James Holden on the Great Eastern Railway. 'Gladstone' class No. 198 *Sheffield* was the last of a small group of engines to have to have its equipment removed in September 1904.

His bold decision to adopt the Schmidt superheater has already been described. Marsh recognised the value of an arrangement wherein the steam pipe was carried as a coil around the interior of the smokebox, and had carried out some experiments of his own, though the results do not appear to have been recorded. He went on to carry out particular experiments on individual locomotives. In the autumn of 1907 the Paris Exhibition engine, No. 189 *Edward Blount* was selected for a series of trials with Hammond's patent air heating apparatus, being provided with a completely new smokebox divided into two compartments by means of a horizontal partition placed above the tube ends. Pre-heated air was directed into the firebox entering the set of tubes via drum-like pockets on each side of the upper part of the smokebox to be warmed by the smokebox gases. The anticipated economy was not realised due to heat loss by the pre-heated air between smokebox and firebox, and the apparatus was disconnected but not removed in 1908, going for scrap with the engine at the end of 1912.

In May 1910 a spare boiler was fitted to 4-4-0 No. 53 *Richmond* incorporating a Hotchkiss water-circulator contained in a second dome just behind the chimney. Accumulated deposits were discharged automatically by means of a blow off pipe, and the removal of the various impurities meant that a boiler

Billinton 'B4' class No. 53 *Richmond* (originally named *Sirdar*) was fitted with a Hotchkiss water circulator in the leading dome on the barrel just behind the chimney. What had served well in stationary boilers did not produce a similar result on an active locomotive. The apparatus was removed and discarded in August 1915 and the locomotive fitted with an extended smokebox. No. 53 is seen here passing Balham Intermediate with an interesting array of stock, and was reproduced in F. Moore's set of railway photographs.

No. 72 was the Billinton 'B4' selected for fitting with new cylinders and Allen's patent segmented piston rings while in Brighton works in July 1908. It emerged that October and after various teething troubles entered revenue earning service at the start of December. Found to be slightly easier on fuel and water and very free running at speed, it lacked the acceleration from stops of its companion 'B4s'. The Allen rings and tailrods were discarded in April 1914. It is seen here just after the fireman has put on more coal, climbing past Grosvenor Road with a Brighton train.

washout was required every 12 days instead of seven. However, such savings were overcome by higher maintenance costs, and the apparatus was removed and discarded in August 1915. A Billinton experiment using Drummond firebox water tubes fitted to No. 45 *Bessborough* was also brought to a conclusion at the end of Marsh's time when his successor fitted a set of longer wearing and more reliable steel tubes. Bradley concedes that 'Marsh had a very open mind concerning inventions or improvements'.

In July 1908 when 'B4' No. 72 was in Brighton works, he decided to fit new cylinders and Allen's patent segmented piston rings. Again there was no overall balance of advantage and the parts involved were discarded in April 1914. Marsh is also reported to have equipped a 'D1' 0-4-2 with a variable blast, worked off the vertical arm of the reversing shaft so the blast regulated itself according to the degree of the cut-off. While the majority of such experiments did not come off, Marsh was also concerned with more straightforward improvements to the fleet of locomotives he inherited, such as ordering all the replacement boilers for classes 'D1' and 'E1' to be of steel with closed doors on the rear of the two rings and modified Ramsbottom safety valves over the firebox, later substituting them with his own cast-iron flared safety valve casing and more rounded dome cover. In fact a whole host of minor improvements helped the majority of the surviving Stroudley and Billinton locomotives last for another generation or more.

Liveries

Perhaps the most conspicuous piece of experimentation was over locomotive and rolling stock liveries, and implementation of the painted umber recommended by Marsh and approved by the Directors following an inspection at London Bridge on 13th October, 1905 of no less than 12 locomotives in a variety of inexpensive, attractive and hard-wearing liveries. The recommendation was made by the Engine Stock Committee under Marsh's guidance who narrowed the choice to five. They reported as follows:

The Committee inspected two goods tender engines, one painted black with red and white lines, the other black with red lines, and three bogie passenger tender engines, one painted green of the present standard colour for goods engines and two painted umber, one with the name on the engine and the Company's initials on the tender, and the other with arms on the engine and initials on the tender. Marsh said the goods engines were painted much like the LNWR's engines and he recommended the adoption of black with red lines on as being a good wearing colour, cheaper than the present colour and not requiring so much cleaning. He said the umber coloured engines were painted a natural colour which matched the colour now being used for the body of the carriages and recommended the adoption. It would be cheaper than the present colour and would wear better. He did not recommend the green.

The Committee not only confirmed Marsh's recommendations but went on to state that 'engines used for both passenger and goods traffic (for example the 'E4' class) should be painted umber, that each engine should be distinguished

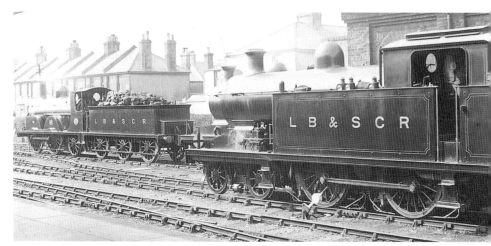

Out of the 14 locomotives lined up for inspection at London Bridge on 13th October, 1905, three featured shades of umber. The passenger livery finally chosen was umber, edged with a darker shade of the same colour, and lined with a black band having a gilt line on either side. Tender locomotives had the tender sides emblazoned with LB&SCR in gilt block letters shaded in black with the company's monogram on the driving wheel splashers, while tank engines had the initials on the tank sides and used a lining of less expensive pale yellow. Examples of both are on view in this F.W. Spry portrait at Littlehampton.

More power was required on certain motor train-serviced lines and Marsh saw an obvious use for some of the ageing 'D' tanks. After several years monitoring motor-fitted No. 232, Marsh went ahead and modified more than 60, commencing with Nos. 605 and 627 in 1909. These had their side tanks lettered 'L & B' in very large characters. This grotesque livery, nicknamed 'Liver and Bacon', failed to gain favour and, on the Chairman's orders, was quickly changed to the standard pattern. It is seen here at Brighton in what has been described as 'sandwich' formation.

in future by a number only, the name being omitted in every case when the engine is repainted and that the coat of arms as painted on the pattern engine should also be omitted'.

The umber was edged with a darker shade of the same colour and lined with a black band having a gilt line on either side, the company's monogram on both driving wheel splashers, while wheels were umber with black boss centres and the interior of the cab painted a stone colour. Despite proving considerably cheaper, the umber wore just as well as Stroudley's yellow and was easier to keep clean, especially in the smoke-ridden atmosphere of the metropolis. Bradley maintains the Stroudley goods green was even better wearing, though turning to almost black after lengthy wear. Certainly the Directors were pleased with the change, cutting almost £6 off the cost of an average Stroudley repaint of £15. The railway journalist Rous-Marten acclaimed the new livery 'a great improvement on the old yellow, which was never pleasing and soon became soiled'.

Costs were cut even further by the decision to remove names and during this period coats-of-arms, while from October 1908 number plates were removed as engines passed through shops, neat transfer numerals proving a less expensive option. Secondary passenger and suburban tank classes in umber livery had a less expensive lining of pale yellow instead of the gilt, and buffer beams of unlined vermilion. The goods classes were painted in a deep glossy well-wearing black with appropriate less expensive lining and yellow lettering and numbering.

The public did not take lying down the removal of the homely locomotive names and golden liveries for the Board Minutes for 7th March, 1906 speak of 'representations from members of the public regarding the discontinuance of the practice of naming engines and the alteration of their colour'. Indeed traditionalists were mightily upset when the splendid new Atlantics appeared not only in umber livery but actually un-named! The General Manager, William Forbes, and locomotive engineer, Earle Marsh were to 'prepare and submit a list of engines or classes of engines which it may be desirable to name, together with a list of names'. But they ordered their previous decision regarding the new livery to be adhered to. On 16th May a list was submitted and 'approved generally subject to addition and omission of certain names to which specific attention was called'. Marsh's mere handful of names was but a sop to Cerberus, enough to pacify outrage until the passing of time mellowed public opinion.

Rebuilds

Late in 1907 Marsh undertook a rebuild of 'B2' class 4-4-0 No. 321 *John Rennie* which initiated the rebuilding of the whole class, and this strategy of improving and upgrading on existing locomotives was infinitely cheaper in comparison than constructing a completely new one. As Bradley perceptively remarked, 'Marsh always disliked scrapping engines if by reboilering or renewal they could undertake more arduous tasks'. This registered with Marsh as the

No. 321 was the first 'B2x' to appear in October 1907. It is seen here in relatively mint condition powering out of Bognor, a classic shot by H. Gordon Tidey. The express, which includes a Pullman car, is headed for Victoria via Horsham and Three Bridges.

The first rebuilt 'C2' was No. 545 which appeared from Brighton works in July 1908, carrying the larger 'C3' boiler with extended smokebox and saddle, completely transforming the insignificant under-boilered Billinton 0-6-0 into a handsome heavy duty engine. In almost as new condition, it was put to work on a heavy goods seen leaving Willow Walk for Brighton, another classic by Gordon Tidey, taken that August.

company entered a period of financial stringency the following year. Ben Webb suggests Marsh's regime was conditioned by the intention of the Board to electrify to Brighton, hence the wisdom of including as much rebuilding of Stroudley and Billinton engines as the construction of new ones of Marsh's own design. Perhaps Marsh's most successful and long lasting decision was to experiment with larger boilers and more modern fittings, a rebuilding process that was to continue right through to the early days of the Southern Railway.

Taking the extensive programme in a chronological sequence, the 'B2' class was first tackled in 1907 in response to complaints from shed foremen that the increased weight of main line services made it difficult to find them suitable duties. Marsh with an ample supply of 'C3' pattern boilers decided to equip the entire class and 'B3' No. 213 *Bessemer* with these as they entered shops for heavy repairs. He had previously considered rebuilding the 'Gladstones' and letting the 'B2s' go for scrap when they needed extensive repairs. However, to rebuild them as inside cylinder 4-4-2s would have cost £1,870 each as against £1,175 to rebuild a 'B2', so he went for the cheaper option. But even this larger boiler was barely adequate as the heating surface still appeared too small to supply steam for fast running. The 25 members with other added modifications were reboilered to 'B2x' from October 1907, and all but three had been converted by the time of Marsh's departure, the last No. 316 *Goldsmid* being rebuilt in July 1916. They were an improvement on the small-boilered engines though not losing their fairly high fuel consumption. A partial success and nothing like the great improvement that had been anticipated, the fundamental trouble lay with the engine rather than the boiler. It was the much-patched up frames which required strengthening on numerous occasions that heralded their demise, the whole class going between December 1929 and November 1932.

The shortcomings of the 'C2s' became apparent when their boilers failed to supply sufficient steam on the 800 ton trains from the GWR to Three Bridges. Marsh therefore had high expectations for his larger 'C3s' were intended to take over the heaviest main line goods duties, but they proved a broken reed in this respect, so he turned back to envision an enhanced 'C2'. He had seen that the two-ring 5 ft boiler when modified behaved admirably and, when united with the successful 'C2' chassis, produced an excellent heavy duty 0-6-0 capable of tackling the most arduous main line goods services. The effect of the large boiler with extended smokebox completely transformed the hitherto insignificant Billinton 0-6-0 to the equal of any contemporary in the country, as haulage test between 'C2x' No. 545 and 'C2' No. 447 in September 1908 indicated. Marsh was responsible for 28 'C2s' that were rebuilt between July 1908 and November 1912. In the end only 10 'C2s' remained unrebuilt, seven being withdrawn in the mid-1930s before they could be rebuilt, and the last 'C2' rebuild took place as late as December 1939. The 'C2s' had gained the nickname 'Vulcans' so not surprisingly the Marsh rebuilds instantly became known as the 'large Vulcans'. The fact that 38 of the rebuilds survived through to the beginning of the 1960s bears testimony, when one considers their ubiquitous performance in coping ably with medium and local goods services across the system, to one of Marsh's outstanding successes.

As with the 'D3s', Marsh had been reboilering members of the 'E4' class with ones of 'I1' pattern but, realising its limitation, decided to fit larger 'I2' boilers

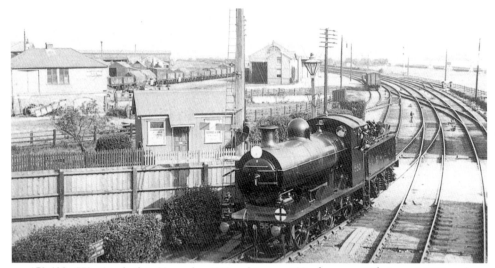

'C2x' No. 550 was rebuilt in November 1910 and is seen at Newhaven on 18th August, 1911, and is leaving the shed exit. Beyond the level crossing the branch for the West Side Quay passes directly behind the little office of Rayner & Son as it and the road in the foreground converge to share the swing bridge over the Ouse. This view taken from the footbridge of Newhaven Town station shows the commodious goods shed besides which stretch a long line of mixed goods wagons.   *R.C. Riley Collection*

A close up detailed view of 'E4x' No. 478, rebuilt in May 1909, and seen standing on New Cross shed. Although in outward appearance these rebuilds had been much enlarged, the heating surface was considerably reduced, inhibiting the steam supply.

experimentally to three 'E4s' in 1909, No. 466 in February and Nos. 478 and 489 in May, becoming class 'E4x'. The graceful Billinton outline was lost, the result producing a somewhat squat and odd looking locomotive. Marsh had been hoping to prevent the accumulation of solid scale behind the front tubeplate but, despite the extra space for circulation, he found himself disappointed, and as a result he installed the company's first water softening plant in Brighton locomotive yard. A fourth 'E4', No. 477, was similarly rebuilt in April 1911. Though an improvement on standard members of the class, the poorly designed valve chests inhibited the more plentiful steam supply. Bradley's appraisal was that 'at £1,500 each they were an expensive luxury and one not repeated'. They appeared predominantly on goods duties and spent lengthy periods yard shunting.

Also in 1909, with his hands tied financially, Marsh decided that as no new boilers were forthcoming, to employ a couple of his spare larger 'I2' boilers on Nos. 396 in April and 397 in June, becoming class 'D3x'. Unfortunately this met with limited success for performance was not improved. The 'I2' boiler had a smaller heating surface but greater water content, resulting in poor steaming and increased fuel consumption, while the higher centre of gravity made running at speed less steady. They were not well received by the locomotive men and were withdrawn well ahead of the majority of the 'D3s', No. 396 in May 1937 and its companion in July 1948. In view of their lack of success, Marsh reverted to fitting the rest of the 'D3s' with smaller 'I1' boilers.

The Stroudley 'D' class 0-4-2 tanks had given sterling service across the system for several decades and, in his search for an improved 'D' tank, Robert Billinton as early as 1892 reboilered seven early members of the class whose boilers badly needed complete overhaul. One of these No. 20 *Carshalton*, renumbered to 79 in February 1907 and 79A in November 1909 to make way for one of the later 'I3s', was singled out by Marsh as the search for an improved version continued, for a second rebuilding. It was stripped to the frames, fitted with a high-pitched Marsh boiler, circular smokebox and saddle, small dome, short chimney and raised cab and emerged from the works on 10th December, 1910. Drivers said it 'waggled' at the front end and rode unsteadily at speed. Plagued by recurrent hot boxes, heavy tyre wear and failing to maintain a good head of steam, it was not a popular engine and met, for a rebuild, a relatively early demise in August 1933. Marsh, perhaps optimistically with hindsight, had six 'D1x' 4 ft 6 in. diameter boilers constructed in 1910. One was used on No. 79A another on No. 89, the 'E1x', one modified for stationary work at Victoria in connection with the electrical plant, another employed on carriage warming at Newhaven, and the remaining pair used at Lancing and sold to the War Department in 1915 which dispatched them to Egypt, in all not the best use of brand new boilers!

At the start of 1911 Marsh decided to utilise some spare 'C3' boilers on four 'E5s', which were fitted with circular smokeboxes and saddles and 'I2' chimneys and became 'E5x'. To contain these large boilers the side tanks of the quartet had to be moved outwards together with other small adaptations which, though producing a large and most impressive looking locomotive, could seldom work to full advantage because the restricted steam-chests

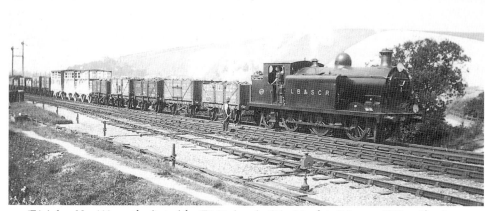

'E4x' class No. 466 was the first of the 'E4s' to be rebuilt by Marsh in February 1909 and has been captured by William Bennett on a goods working out of Lewes East Yard passing Southerham. The stock on view consists of numerous privately-owned colliery wagons and three white lime-coated cattle wagons.   *M.P. Bennett Collection/Bluebell Archives*

No. 489 was rebuilt to class 'E4x' in May 1909, and is glimpsed working a 'stopper' from Victoria, seen entering East Croydon. Bradley writes: 'It may only be an impression but in Brighton days the "E4xs" always appeared to work more than their share of goods duties as well as frequently spending quite lengthy periods yard shunting'.   *Author's Collection*

In April 1909 'D3' No. 396 was turned out of Brighton works rebuilt with a larger boiler of Marsh's design. The smokebox was extended and carried on a saddle. It is seen here at New Cross shed.

'D3x' No. 397 followed in June 1909, and makes a fine portrait by the turntable at Brighton shed. Despite the grand proportions the pair were indifferent steamers, and soon came to be worked on lighter duties.

No. 397 again, photographed by H. Gordon Tidey south of Hassocks on a local service from East Grinstead via Haywards Heath to Brighton. This must have been soon after rebuilding, as the higher centre of gravity made running at speed less steady and probably accounted for their poor reception by the enginemen.

Marsh had been toying for some time with the idea of upgrading the ageing Stroudley 'D' tanks, providing No. 20 *Carshalton* with one of his high-pitched boilers, a circular smokebox and saddle, a small dome and taller cab. J.N. Maskelyne relates how its ungainly appearance was facetiously referred to as 'a fat little fellow with his mammy's eyes', taken from a song of the period! Unsteadiness on the road, despite the weight of a heavy cast-iron drag plate below the footplate, left the renumbered 79A a solitary rebuild. Based at West Croydon, the shed which had the only fitter with sufficient expertise to attend to it, it is seen here at East Croydon.

'E5' No. 570 was rebuilt with a Marsh 'C3' boiler and reappeared in new condition in March 1911. The weaknesses mentioned in his previous rebuilds remained, though not to such an extent and the four converted 'E5Xs' all completed their half-century. No. 570 poses for its official photograph on the Crumbles line where a pocket of the winter's snow still lingers on.

frequently resulted in the front end becoming choked. The high centre of gravity and greater weight at the front also made running at speed noticeably less even while fuel consumption proved higher. These locomotives in question were No. 586 (January), 570 (March), 401 (May) and 576 (July). Surprisingly they outlasted most of their unrebuilt class members, No. 32570 being amongst the final survivors to go at the beginning of 1956.

In 1906 the reboilering of the 'Terriers' had been considered but no decision reached. Marsh returned to the idea of upgrading the power of the humble but sprightly Stroudley 'Terriers' to cope with the increasing loads of the motor train services. Twelve new boilers were to be built at Brighton works over the following 12 months to his own design with the barrel constructed in one ring. A circular extended smokebox resting on a saddle was provided together with new pattern steam-operated sandboxes placed beneath the footplate. Though this was not put into effect by the time of Marsh's resignation, a baker's dozen of 'A1s' were fitted as per Marsh's instruction to class 'A1x' between November 1911 and December 1913, the extra one being made available to *Fenchurch*, owned by the Newhaven Harbour Company following its sale by the LB&SCR for £360 in June 1898. According to Bradley, 'Those reboilered received a long new lease of life, for the 'A1x' boiler was found to be as good, if not a better steamer than the original Stroudley pattern in its prime, as well as being unusually light on maintenance'. No wonder that Lawson Billinton was content to continue to have Marsh boilers built as required. Their future well secure, the 'Terriers' soldiered on through both World Wars, at the end of the second of which just two members, the former No. 54 *Waddon* and No. 82 *Boxhill* remained as 'A1s' to join eight 'A1x' into preservation, a testimony not only to their popularity but to the fact that they had survived so many adventures and narrow escapes on the way.

In the light of his earlier experiment with 'Terriers' as 2-4-0Ts, Marsh realised that a more powerful 'A' class locomotive was required for handling the heavier loaded motor trains. No. 677 was the first of a long line of survivors to be reboilered in November 1911 under instructions given by Marsh that March, and is seen at Tunbridge Wells shed.

Marsh selected 'E1' class No. 89 for rebuilding as an 'E1x' with a boiler of similar pattern to that used on his 'D1x'. In addition new side tanks, bunker and cab were provided. However, an order of May 1912 forbad its use on all passenger duties because of unsteadiness at speed when passing crossovers or round curves. West Croydon was its second posting and the location here is near Waddon Marsh. No. 89 was a rare example of a rebuild being reconverted to the original, and it re-emerged as an 'E1' in March 1930, lasting till 1960.

In January 1911 Marsh took 'E1' 0-6-0T No. 89 *Brest* into works as a guinea pig for reboilering all the class. It left shops on 10th June wearing a 'D1x' boiler and carrying new square-topped tanks, in all a robust good-looking shunting tank (class 'E1x'). However, unsteadiness at speed at crossovers or round curves saw it banned from all passenger duties, for the 'E1s' on occasions took their turn on services, to the Dyke to name one instance. The rebuilding cost of £1,480 was seen to be hardly worth it and explains why no other 'E1s' received similar attention. The Southern Railway must have deemed it worthwhile to reverse the experiment and reconvert it to an 'E1' in March 1930, for it soldiered on into early 1960 before being broken up.

The 'E6' class was Robert Billinton's last design which he sadly never saw completed as the first three members came out a month after his death. Marsh was left to complete the class. The last pair, Nos. 417 and 418, were to have been 0-8-0 shunting tanks for the marshalling yards at Willow Walk and Lower Yard, Brighton respectively. Both Marsh and the Chief Engineer disliked the scheme, Marsh considering eight-coupled tanks an unnecessary luxury for such duties and was averse to having two odd members of a class. The final pair emerged retaining the special side rods of heavy 'H' section, but as 0-6-2Ts like the others. It was with these relatively new six-year-old locomotives that Marsh chose to experiment using a 'C3' boiler, selecting Nos. 407 and 411 for reboilering in June and November 1911 respectively, becoming class 'E6x'. They received almost identical treatment to the 'E5' conversions, but did not suffer from cramped valve chests and could take full advantage of the greater steam supply and improved adhesion, outclassing their unaltered classmates. Bradley describes them as 'undoubtedly the best radial tanks owned by the Company'. All the same, they took turn about with their fellow 'E6s' on South London goods workings when they were based first at New Cross and later at Norwood, and were among the early withdrawals of the class in the late 1950s.

Summary

Marsh was responsible for the rebuilding of 78 locomotives ordered during his regime across a wide range of classes, and further 'Terriers' (nine including Kent & East Sussex Railway No. 3 in April 1943) and 'C2s' (17) continued to be altered along identical lines well into the Southern Railway days. Discounting his completion of Billinton's 12 'E6' tanks which were underway at the time he took over, and allowing for the delivery of 'I3s' and the 'J' No. 326 finished under his successor Lawson Billinton, Marsh rebuilt almost as many locomotives as the 85 of his own design, a tremendous programme for the 6½ years in charge at Brighton, at the end of which he left the Department so well endowed that, with Lawson Billinton's limited building programme prior to the Great War, the LB&SCR had ample motive power to see it through the war years. Once again, as with the 'I' tank classes, the results were chequered; from dismal failures which performed below the standard of the unrebuilt members to scintillating successes, especially with the 'A1x', 'C2x' and 'E6x' rebuilds. At least he could be said to have been brave enough to experiment - and even failed experiments are part of the learning curve. But in all too many cases he was forced to cut his losses and curtail his programme of rebuilds.

No. 407 was the first 'E6' rebuild to appear in July 1911, and proved one of the few successful class conversions undertaken by Marsh. Whether this can be classed as an official photograph or not, the background of the downland hills at the neck of Lewes East goods sidings provide a fitting setting. Another F. Moore card photograph.

The other 'E6x' was No. 411 which appeared in November 1911. The gentleman standing in the cab at New Cross has a distinct likeness to D.E. Marsh, but this is wishful thinking. He had left the scene by this late date, and the photographer, O.J. Morris, did not commence his railway photography until 1919.

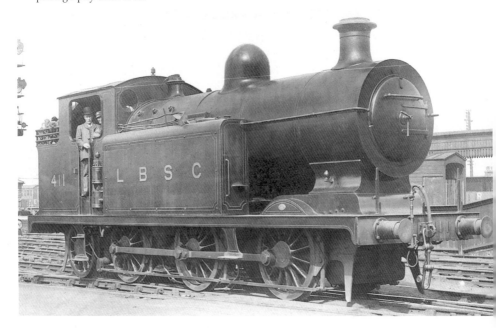

Chapter Four

Instructions

From the foregoing chapter it might be assumed that Marsh was chiefly preoccupied with the construction, rebuilding and repair of the company's locomotives and rolling stock. However, a file survives at the National Archives (Rail 414 260/1) with the description *Extract from Minutes and Board Orders* directed to the locomotive and carriage superintendent. It consists of directives, issued by the Board not merely from the Directors' Meetings but from all the company's numerous departments and working committees, over which action was required from the superintendent. Each extract is headed 'D.E. Marsh', stamped in purple ink, and ends with the stamped signature of the company's Secretary, Mr Brewer. Going through this ledger, one is perusing these pasted up directives that would have landed on Marsh's desk and which, unless he was a member of the relevant committee, he would be seeing for the first time. The sheer volume of requirements presents a picture of an extremely hard-worked man for, although much could be delegated down the line, all decisions and action needed to come from the man at the top.

The Reconstruction of Brighton Works

Probably the most time consuming matter that occupied Marsh throughout his superintendence was the rebuilding of Brighton works with all its accompanying problems. Plans were still being redrawn while the work was underway. In March 1907 Marsh conducted an inspection of certain shops and explained the proposals already sanctioned for extensions. The report reads: 'His present intention was that in addition to the work in extending the Smith's Shop, the present Carriage Shop at Preston shall be converted into a running shed'. He was linking up the vacation of the carriage shop with the fact that space at Brighton shed was becoming inadequate. He had earlier in October 1905 directed attention to 'the Running Shed which can accommodate 40 engines, whilst 100 have to be stabled at Brighton.' He had proposed to convert the wagon repair shop into a running shed and take over the cattle docks adjacent to the present running shed for the purpose of coal stages, subject to the approval of the goods manager. In 1908 in the light of reduced working hours for the works staff, he was proposing 'Improved office accommodation for the Locomotive Department at Brighton (£1,500), the erection of a new Mess Room and Pay and Time offices in the Locomotive Works (£3,300)' as part of a drive towards improved timekeeping of a staff that often took liberties. Marsh was still changing his mind late in that year, recommending the cupola stage of the altered foundry be remodelled and laid in the bottom of the foundry.

Then there were problems of reorganisation during the rebuilding. The stores in the works area were relocated to Newhaven. There was the obvious disruption to the working staff and to them the unwelcome unemployment

The derailment of recently ex-works 'D' class No. 239, which lost its name *Patcham* in March 1907, is the centre of interest. To the right on the same track are the lead vehicles of the breakdown train. Behind the recently painted fencing of the lengthy cattle dock stand two Billinton horse boxes contrasting with the Stroudley example in centre picture. This scene was to be transformed into a new coaling stage area opposite the turntable in left background. Coaling by two cranes was till then being provided to the south of the large water tower where, as can be seen in the top right-hand corner, the new Desrumaux system water softening plant was installed. *Author's Collection*

The fan of lines in the south yard of Brighton works which led towards the iron foundry, hence the several wagons loaded with coke and coal. Looking north (*from the left*) would be the engineer's department, boiler shop, cylinder and wheel shop, and the smith's shop, showing wooden scaffolding at the points where the various buildings were to be extended.

without compensation when their shops were dismantled, though these financial savings suited the hard-strapped company. At long last on 12th October, 1910 the General Manager was able to report 'the whole of the work of altering the Locomotive shops is now complete'.

During this lengthy period Marsh was responsible for the identification and ordering of all new equipment and machinery and the list, let alone the expense, is quite awesome. Marsh had to tender for all the required iron and steel work, much of it in girders, which was to swallow up the area of the yard south of the smith's shop.

Some of the more imposing pieces of equipment ordered included two turntables for the works, a patent portable crucible furnace, a 30 cwt crane and girders for wheel and frame fitting shops (from Cravens), a hydraulic accumulator, a universal milling machine and a vertical milling and copying machine (from Messrs Smith & Coventry), hydraulic riveting apparatus, a portable cylinder boring machine with pneumatic motor (from Cravens) and two sets of pumps to work the well in the Brighton shops (from Messrs Tangye), together with a host of compressors, cranes, lathes and drilling machines.

The above-mentioned pumps and the experience of going down the well shaft are recalled by Bert Perryman in *When Steam was King at Brighton* (pages 93-4):

Brighton works had its own water supply drawn from its own well about 120 ft deep. Two sets of triple standpipe pumps (one in use and one stand-by) were located in an 'engine room' below floor level in the north end of the old smith's shop and immediately above the borehole proper. Long rods, supported by wooden guide blocks fastened to the well sides, led the drive downwards from the three throw crankshafts to the actual pumps, which were located in the 'wet headings', about 112 ft down. A vertical steel ladder, attached to the side of the well, gave access to the headings.

The areas of Heat and Lighting were vital to the modernisation of the works. Heating apparatus was to be provided in the erecting and machine shops and in the paint and trimming shops. Marsh had to attend to contracts for water, for gas and oil and coal. With regards to oil the choice of grade was vital, for example with engine and cylinder oil. But the greatest step forward was the introduction of electric power for working the machinery, and Marsh had to negotiate with the Brighton Corporation regarding the supply of electric energy. He had to make purchases of motors, switchboards (from the British Westinghouse Electric & Manufacturing Company) together with a host of other electrical equipment. But even in small but vital contracts such as finding the right rubber for hosepipes and meeting the stipulation that 'only the best quality varnish shall be used for new stock', Marsh had to pay close attention to detail.

The reconstruction of the Brighton works was for Marsh a notable achievement, even more coping with the disruption to locomotive repairs and the temporary laying off of a large part of the workforce during this period. The site was rebuilt to the greatest extent possible so that when considering its future in 1960, the recommendation was for closure for 'it proved impossible to extend the Works due to its hillside location and proximity of the lines into Brighton Station'. It had been suggested in Marsh's time that the locomotive works might also be resited alongside the new carriage works at Lancing, but the intervention of World War I halted the scheme.

The boiler house at Brighton works, which contains on the left a beam engine used to bring up water. There was at least one well shaft, possibly more. The engine house wall is already broken through, indicating pending replacement by an electric generator. On the right are two Craven boilers which provided power for fans supplying air to the smith's shop. Photograph taken *c.* 1908.

Workers stand by the lathes in the Lancing wheel shop *c.* 1910. These were designed for machinery and turning of wheels on one axle, and were operated by auxiliary belts driven from pulleys above on a long shaft. Seen here are 3 ft 7½ in. carriage wheels with on the left another axle ready to be turned. It was dangerous work, and the fearsome foreman seen with his hands on his lapels was there to enforce care and discipline. *Philip Fry Collection*

Lancing

As if all the stress connected with the reconstruction of Brighton was not enough, Marsh found himself at the same time closely involved in the setting up of the new carriage and wagon works at Lancing. On 29th January, 1905 a 96½ acre site of virtually flat land to the south-west of Lancing station was purchased from the Carr-Lloyd Estate for £21,683 2s. 6d. Early in November 1905 he was party to negotiations with Lord Leconfield regarding the use of land on the new site. A year later the question of a supply of water for the works came up and, alongside the company's Engineer, he was instructed to either conduct borings or negotiate a supply from Brighton Corporation. He had to take note of the Rolling Stock Committee's plans for Lancing together with the costings.

In July 1906 defects in the roof of a 'Balloon' trailer due to the use of unseasoned wood was queried by the Directors who received an answer that the company possessed no accommodation for the proper storage and seasoning of timber, and a note was made to provide such at Lancing. In the following October it was agreed to 'build saw mills and provide a timber stacking yard and shed at Lancing, and the laying on of sidings for the breaking of carriage stock'. Slowly but surely the complex came to include in addition to the main repair shop, used from 1910 solely for carriage construction, a wheel turning and machine shop, power house, saw mill and timber drying shed. At the end of 1908 the iron and steel work for Lancing was ordered from Dorman Long & Co. at a cost of £7,893, and the following spring he was proposing the installation of the Fiddian system of treating sewerage at Lancing carriage works. That summer the equipment was ordered, including two cranes at £1,640, diesel engines, dynamos and a spring making machine. In 1910 a steam drying plant and accompanying chimney stack was ordered. Marsh was already *hors de combat* on 25th May, 1911 when a visit of inspection found the carriage shop virtually completed, though Messrs Billinton and Panter both complained of delay caused by non-delivery of diesel engines.

Electrification

Another huge project under Marsh's aegis was the South London electrification, hinted at in March 1905 when the importance of the locomotive returnd sent in by Marsh were underlined 'in view of possible development of electric traction and motor car services'. By 1906 Marsh was with Dawson involved in negotiating contracts for the electric equipment. At the end of 1908 it was the shops and sidings at Peckham Rye that engaged his attention and late in 1910 Marsh was fretting over the delay by the Allgemeine Company of delivery of stock equipment for the South London Line.

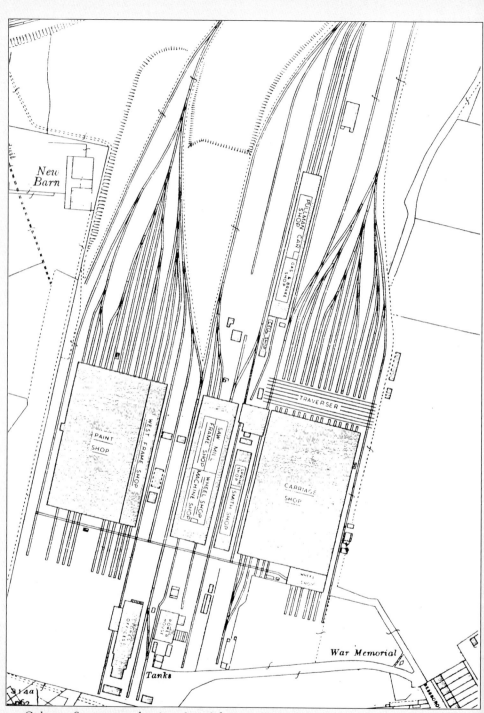

New
Barn

PULLMAN CAR SHOP

GAS & STORES

TRAVERSER

WEST FRAME SHOP

PAINT
SHOP

SAW MILL
FRAME SHOP

WHEEL SHOP
MACHINE SHOP

SMITH SHOP

CARRIAGE
SHOP

WHEEL
SHOP

Tanks

War Memorial

Ordnance Survey map showing plan of the completed Lancing carriage works in 1931. The building on the right started as the wagon shop but was soon given over to carriage construction and repairs.

The original smithy building was constructed of corrugated iron sheeting on a steel frame, and located alongside the original building. At the several furnaces the metal fittings were all fabricated on site, ranging from large leaf springs and body strapping to the smallest of hinges. The foreman on the right casts a baleful stare towards the camera. The picture was taken around 1912. At a later stage the shop was rebuilt in brick. *Philip Fry Collection*

The first wagon was outshopped at the new Lancing works on 13th April, 1909. Surrounded by members of the works staff is No. 715, an 8 ton open 'A' wagon which is yet to have its tare weight painted on. Several photographs exist of this red letter occasion in the history of the LB&SCR Co. *Colin Paul Collection*

The First Wagon – Lancing – 13 April 1909.

The pristine quality of the new Lancing works is seen soon after opening. The white-railed entrance road leads past the grounded bodies of a Stroudley third brake and a covered carriage truck to reveal the original main building, later to become the carriage shop, with a wheel shop (*left*) at its seaward end. A closer examination reveals various items of stock in the background from gas containers to stationary boilers, more grounded bodies and even an SECR wagon.   *John Minnis Collection*

Carriage & Wagon Matters

The ordering of locomotive parts such as superheaters on the Schmidt's system and the piston valves that necessarily accompanied them were Marsh's bread and butter, but he was also responsible for vetting all orders of the carriage and wagon sections. Only three months into his job he ordered several 20 ton trucks on trial and at the end of 1907 placed an order for 500 wagons. In June 1905 he was ready to go ahead with the proposal to build 37 new coaches, 16 of them with much-welcomed lavatory accommodation at an estimate cost of £28,000. In October he confirmed six bogie lavatory carriages for the Eastbourne Express. In July he was ordering switches for lathes at Preston Park carriage works. In November he made the innovative purchase of a vacuum carriage cleaner plant at Eardley depot in Streatham, and floated a revolutionary proposal for the LB&SCR to build Pullmans of their own to replace those of the Pullman Car Company. In this he was slapped down by the Board who agreed to renew their agreement from 31st December for a seven year term, the Pullman Car Company to bear one-third of the cost of maintenance and renewal of bodies, etc. Even this was not straightforward. The Pullman Car Company objected but the Board refused to waive their condition. In the end the following May the former offered £200 towards the costs, and this was accepted.

At the end of 1905 Marsh conducted a series of trials with a new automatic system of carriage lighting with ordinary gas and incandescent burners which were in use on the Western of France Railway. As a result five gas holders were purchased from the District Railway and four hired at 30s. per week from the Metropolitan. Orders for steel bogies and steel carriage underframes passed through Marsh's hands. He was accountable for carriage lighting and monitoring gas consumption. He was expected to know something about oak wagon 'scantling' (timber less than 5 in. in breadth and thickness). In 1907 he looked at a proposal by Mr Davison Daiziel, Chairman of the Pullman Car Company, proposing additional Pullman cars of an improved type to be placed on special services to Brighton and Eastbourne, and to Portsmouth. This was taken up with the idea of the new train, entirely British-built supplanting the 'Pullman Limited'. The end result was the famous 'Southern Belle', inaugurated on 1st November, 1908 to a 60 minute schedule, making two journeys on Sunday, extended to weekdays on 1st June, 1909 and exactly a year later made a further two additional trips daily. The former 'Pullman Limited' stock was transferred to the Eastbourne service, but although two of the 1899 magnificent 12-wheeled cars had been named *The Arundel* and *The Chichester*, they did not run to Portsmouth until much later and then as single cars, the 1909 timetable showing them only running as far as Bognor via Worthing.

Other Matters

Although the province of stations was strictly under the company's Engineer, where matters related to locomotives and rolling stock the locomotive superintendent's opinion was of paramount importance. In April 1906, for instance, Marsh ordered a pump and electric motor for draining the turntable and pits at Victoria from Gwynnes Ltd, at £88 15s., and delivery took place in October. Soon after that Marsh was instructed to carry out a revaluation of Victoria and the line of railway, and then to comment on the proposal to erect shops and offices along the station frontage at Eastbourne.

When it came to engine sheds Marsh had full control. In March 1907 he accepted the offer from Messrs Bowes, Scott and Western to erect a water softening plant on the Desrumaux system at Brighton for £2,750 with a further £750 for excavation, rearranging the mains and for masonry, etc. Water softening apparatus was also ordered later for Victoria and London Bridge. In August 1906 it had been noted that the water available at Battersea was unsuitable. Early in 1909 an analysis of the water used there showed it to be unfit for boilers. Marsh was ordered to obtain water at the cost of £1,000 after £620 had already been written off in boring and drainage works to try and remedy the situation.

At the end of 1906 he ordered three turntables from Ransome and Rapier Ltd, for £1,323 that were large enough to accommodate the new Atlantics, and gave orders the following autumn for a new engine shed at Midhurst 'to be paved and that smoke stacks be provided at a cost of £130, then for a coal stage and siding to be extended and altered at Battersea Yard for £2,400, and for a new shed at Eastbourne to hold 24 locomotives'. This was completed in 1911/12 and was, according to Roger Griffiths, 'without question the best laid out of all LB&SCR sheds with ample room for men and machines'. Just a year earlier Marsh had seen the new locomotive shed at Three Bridges brought to completion.

In 1907 Marsh saw to it that the roof of Brighton shed was renovated at a cost of £1,415. Late that year it was felt improvements were necessary to the running shed and locomotive yard at New Cross, but proposals were cancelled in May 1908. But both new and repair work was queuing up and there was no room to house 56 tank engines. A new shed was 'now to be constructed at Norwood Junction at an estimate of £23,622', a case of remarkable foresight as Norwood shed only materialised a quarter of a century later in 1935. In March 1909 he ordered the purchase of two 30 cwt jib coaling steam cranes at Eastbourne and New Cross to replace their predecessors which were beyond repair. Also for the locomotive shops at the latter shed in order to introduce electric working, he ordered an electrically-driven air compressor. Early in 1911 the roof of the paint shop at Brighton was repaired at a cost of £700, and a few months later the roofs of two of the New Cross engine sheds were to be repaired at an estimate of £400.

And this was by no means the end of Marsh's job description. An ongoing monthly stipulation was the 'Returns'. He had to submit sets for punctuality of trains, frequently laid at the door of the Locomotive Department if trains were late, and many invariably were. He had when specifically requested to submit updates on numbers of engines in traffic, under repair and awaiting repairs. He had to report on the progress or non-completion of various works in his Department. He had to prepare regular returns of the amount paid in wages at the Brighton shops each half-year and have them compared with the previous half-year. Naturally Marsh left the groundwork to number crunchers lower down the departmental ladder, but these returns still demanded his careful attention and examination. He was also continually negotiating engine coal rates with Stephenson Clarke & Co., the company's chosen supplier.

Marsh had to sort out cases of indiscipline throughout his department such as cases of theft by staff of such items as carriage cushions or from passengers luggage in transit. He had often to hear these cases personally. He came down heavily on sharp practice such as the case of workmen obtaining promotion and piecework wages who had been making payments to the foreman. The latter, by the name of David Thomson, was dismissed for gross misconduct.

There were also two awkward spheres that required Marsh's frequent attention. Each year there were a dozen or more men incapacitated at work, in shed areas and other railway premises, or in the course of their duties, including a number whose accidents were fatal.

Brighton works was a dangerous place to work in during an era where no real health and safety policy existed. Cases of compensation from the railway company were numerous and time consuming.

The other was over excessive smoke emissions, particularly most frequently in the inner London suburban area around the London termini. Tower Bridge, Bermondsey and Greenwich Police Courts were the most frequently attended where the representatives of the company had to explain their enginemen's transgressions to the new muscle-flexing London County Council which sought punitive fines.

Marsh was also embroiled in the fatal injury to William Zeitz at Stoats Nest in April 1907 where the station master, John Bromley, had permitted him and his film company 'to be upon the premises of the Company for unauthorised

The Stoats Nest disaster of 29th January, 1910 involving the 3.40 pm, Brighton-Victoria express. Shown is the lifting under the arc lights at night of lavatory third No. 1325 which had turned over, having parted company with its culprit bogies and, after mounting the platform ramp, slid along the platform to come to rest nearly broadside on to the line, eventually blocking all four roads.

purpose'. As locomotive superintendent Marsh was asked to deal with driver William Pogmore who was also implicated in the affair.

Traffic accidents naturally received his close attention. To quote just one example, on 21st August, 1905 a light engine, 'B2' 4-4-0 No. 320, collided with a train of empty carriages between Preston Park and Brighton causing the blocking of up and down lines with consequent delay to traffic. The cost of damages to carriages and the locomotive amounted to £464 11s. 6d. Both driver and fireman were to blame and were suspended from duty for a week with loss of pay, and reduced to goods men with decreased pay. In major cases like the Stoats Nest disaster of 29th January, 1910 when 7 people were killed, 42 injured and 10 hospitalised, Marsh was called upon to give evidence at the subsequent enquiry.

One of the requirements demanded of the locomotive superintendent was the supervision of the student apprentices at the Brighton Municipal Technical College. He had to make up an approved list and allocate a sum of £50 for the purchase of the end of year prizes. He also had to nominate representatives of his staff to the Conciliation Boards of which there were three in his Department, the Locomotive Department Northern and Southern Districts and the Department overall. Sitting on the latter was a Director, the General Manager, Marsh himself, the district locomotive superintendents for North and South, and the carriage superintendent.

Such was the weightload of supervisory work demanded of the Brighton's locomotive, carriage and wagon superintendent. If men like Marsh and Wainwright, his contemporary on the SECR, holding so many reins, cracked under the strain, it was no surprise to see in both cases their Board Directors detach the carriage and wagon sector from the locomotive superintendent's over-stretched domain. It came too late to save Marsh.

Not 'Single' *Abergavenny* moving out of Lewes, where the prison buildings loom large on the western fringes of the town, but a photograph of a Stroudley 'Lyons' class 0-4-2 getting to grips with the grades up to Falmer tunnel where No. 325 had come to a stop in heavy rain, signing the class's execution. Though the postcard is dated DE 23 09, all the 'D2s' had been withdrawn by July 1906, several lingering on in the locomotive store sidings at Horsted Keynes till the following year.

Chapter Five

Interaction

Man Management

To understand Marsh's turbulent relationship with the men under his supervision, it is necessary to examine his character and temperament. Both contemporary comments and incidents can assist in their delineation.

A.B. MacLeod, who was an employee and later an authority on the Brighton, mentioned that Marsh was unpopular on arrival, all too frequently the case when a new broom takes over, and Marsh himself sensed this antipathy at the outset lecturing a delegation from Brighton works that 'when he had only been there two days, they wished to remove him'. Philip Evetts writes. 'He was not close to his men who had no good to say of him. Behind his back the men called him "a bloody rogue" and were hard on him throughout'. The late Bernard Nevers of Heathfield, who knew him well, described Marsh as 'unreliable'. Ben Webb summarised Marsh's time at Brighton as follows: 'Though his regime was brief it was drastic. He was a brilliant engineer but outside his field he was brusque and unpredictable'.

More to the point there are a number of incidents recorded which help to explain the rough ride Marsh experienced in his dealings with both colleagues and rank and file railway staff. He was possessed of an uncertain temper and irritability. Evetts recalls hearing of the flaming rows over lost time on trains and especially the instance of the Royal train almost coming to a stop on the way to Epsom Downs, one of his underpowered 'I' tanks being the culprit. He was known to have a short fuse; these traits, coupled with a knee jerk reaction proved explosive on numerous occasions.

He was both officious and peremptory as, on the occasion when he visited Battersea depot. David (Dan) Archer, who began his apprenticeship in 1904 at Battersea where his father was in charge during Marsh's time, tells how the latter came to the sheds one day and, after a tour of inspection, shocked Dan's father by declaring: 'You've got too many men here, Archer. Sack some of them!' Marsh may, perhaps, have been under some pressure from his Directors, asserting on one occasion: 'The Company is managed for the interests of the shareholders . . . and on a commercial basis', and on another, 'As a matter of £.s.d. we cannot waste money'. However, Archer was acutely dismayed. He was always concerned for the welfare of his men, and he felt that Marsh was being utterly callous, without a thought for the hardship which was bound to result from his order, in many cases affecting employees who had been working for the company for many many years in an era when jobs were for life. Marsh must have been displeased by John Archer's attitude, for in November 1905 he recommended his removal from district superintendent at Battersea to assistant shed foreman at Brighton, and attached an initialled directive: 'Alteration of rate carries'.

Another example of Marsh's instant and irrevocable reaction is related by Bradley, Maskelyne and J.E. Kite. No exact date is given but the incident must

109

have occurred late in 1906 or the early part of 1907. 'G' class No. 325 *Abergavenny* had just come off the 3.45 pm from Victoria at Tunbridge Wells, but a shortage of available engines resulted in the 'Single' being called upon immediately to work a train to Brighton via Lewes, a line of severe gradients and awkward curves. After a few trying moments caused by torrential rain Lewes was reached, but the veteran stalled on Falmer Bank and could not be persuaded to go any further, a combination of freak adverse weather conditions and slipping on rails rendered treacherous by rainswept leaves. Now it so happened that Marsh was travelling by that train. Incensed by the slipping and exasperated by the loss of time, on reaching his office the next day he gave orders for No. 325 and all its classmates to be withdrawn and sold for scrap. There were no mechanical grounds for this decision and J.E. Kite in his book *Vintage Steam* is firmly of the opinion that, but for this incident, the class might have lasted longer.

Withdrawals commenced in the summer of 1907 and by the end of the year the great majority of the Stroudley 'G' class 'Singles', many fitted with new boilers by Robert Billinton between 1899 and 1902, and with a great deal of life still left in them, had gravitated to the open air store at Horsted Keynes, and eventually to scrap. No 'Single' was ever to carry the new Marsh livery. L.E. Brailsford goes even further in saying that Marsh going in 1911 'saved the lives of many of Stroudley's engines, as it became evident he considered them out of date'.

Labour Relations

Marsh had taken up his new duties in January 1905, bringing with him a strong breeze from Doncaster, and it was not long before he made his presence felt. He tried to reform Brighton works on the successful lines he had known at Doncaster. Not only did what held good at the latter not work out, but it incurred the resentment of the Brighton workforce. Marsh did not help matters by stating soon after he arrived that he wished to take every possible step to stop overtime work. E.J. Tyler, an employee at Brighton works, relates how Marsh 'brought with him from Doncaster many new ideas which tended to disrupt the friendly atmosphere which had prevailed in the Works during the term of the previous Chief. As a result some of the older officials resigned and were replaced by men from outside'. Sweeping changes were made both in organisation and personnel, and many key men like L.S. Smart, the works manager, sensing an ill wind on the blow, resigned in February and left for the Central South African Railway. The new works manager, Walter Alexander, appointed in March from Kerr, Stuart & Co., proved somewhat too efficient for many of the older men who thereupon resigned and were replaced by newcomers, some from Doncaster and a few from Swindon where Marsh had previously been assistant works manager. Indeed in May one of the last of the Stroudleys in LB&SCR employment was relieved of his duty of inspecting locomotive stores and material from northern manufacturers. F.W. Stroudley declined an inferior position at Brighton and left.

Another key body of up and coming men, the works apprentices, also found themselves nursing a considerable grievance. It had been the custom to allow the senior lads of the erecting shop to go out on footplate runs on engines during their trial trips after overhaul. Premium apprentices could furthermore choose to spend their last six months as firemen on all classes of traffic. Both these privileges were now withdrawn, causing disappointment and resentment. In May 1905 it was stipulated that six was to be the maximum number of apprentices at a £50 premium.

Very little direct documentation concerning Marsh has survived but very fortunately in the PRO at Kew is a file entitled 'Staff Meetings with the Locomotive Engineer' (RAIL 414 758), subtitled 'Copy of the memoranda of the meetings held between the Locomotive Engineer and delegates appointed by the staff'. These record the trouble and strife within Brighton works together with negotiations with the enginemen. These minutes appear to be verbatim, taken down in shorthand by a secretary before being written or typed up. This means that one is actually seeing on record the live utterances of D.E. Marsh as Fred Rich, who first trawled the files, puts it - 'maybe the next best thing to meeting him'.

Marsh was unfortunate to be in the harness at a time when the budding Trades Union movement was beginning to flex its muscles, and the arena of Brighton works was no exception. The pot had been simmering for several years until the lid was blown off by a strike of boilermakers on 24th May, 1905. The bane of Marsh's life at Brighton was undoubtedly the militants in the boiler shop who gave him trouble all the way through.

Duel with the Boilermakers 1905

First in the file are four sets of documents relating to this strike lodged in the folder with a covering slip 'Memorandum June 1906 with Mr Macrae's compliments' (the latter was one of the Brighton Directors). The first is a report of a meeting on 26th May between Marsh, W. Alexander (works manager) and Mr Richards (delegate for the Boilermakers Society). The proceedings were a veritable duel with prolonged cut and thrust between the combatants. Quoting from these proceedings sheds considerable light on aspects of Marsh's character, but first the background to the strike, which was in the nature of a demarcation dispute, best explained by Mr Bennett, a foreman boilermaker, who was called in early on. Marsh asked him to 'describe the incident that sent the men out of the shop, how they threw down their tools'.

Bennett explained how he had a man stopped out who had been using a pneumatic hammer. He had shifted another man to this job and now had to look for a replacement in turn. He found Pelling, the young man in fault, and put him on the job (Pelling was earning 24s. per week). 'He came to me afterwards and said he was not a full paid man.' I said, 'There is no objection I think to your working on a job of this sort'. He was an apprentice who had served his time and become a journeyman. Then two men came saying they were a deputation from the men as regards shifting Pelling on this work.

The faces of the boilermakers' workforce appear in this fine view of the interior of the shop, showing the many varied pieces of machinery. Taken in Edwardian times, these men were very likely to be amongst those who on several successive occasions downed their tools. The vast expanse of the boiler shop displays a variety of work and equipment. Of interest on the right side is a junction of the trolley line. All the staff wear flat caps. This photograph was taken from a high position on the wall of the shop, and comes from an album of H.M. Madgwick's collection in the possession of the author.

The boiler shop at Brighton works showing a long line of boilers receiving attention. It was the militant boilermen who gave Marsh an extremely hard time with their 'trade union' militancy over the threat to reform longstanding working practices. The narrow gauge trolley line runs between the lines of boilers.

'Would I shift him off?' Bennett told them to see Mr Marsh or Mr Alexander, so they went away at that, but came back to ask permission for time off at night to have a meeting. 'I said I could not see my way clear to grant this, on account of pressure of work.' The majority nevertheless took time off. Next morning they came in and said 'What are you going to do about that man? Are you going to shift him?' I said, 'No, for the present.' and advised work till breakfast time and then send a deputation to Mr Marsh. The representatives went away to tell the men, returned and told that if the men's demands were not acceded to, they would down tools. I said, 'I am sorry you are taking a course like this which I do not think is justified'.

The meeting had opened with Richards asking whether Marsh would like to see a deputation of the men. 'They would prefer this question to be discussed, it would be better for the men to be here.' Marsh explained that he had communicated with the Boilermakers Society headquarters 'because all our men are members and because they took such a high handed proceeding as leaving their work without reason, without giving any notice or sending a deputation to me'.

R   Of course they state they applied for a deputation to see someone, and were refused.

M   Instead of taking the Foreman's advice they threw down their tools and went out.

R   That is why I think it would be better to have the deputation if you would not mind so that you can hear what they told us.

M   I am telling you what actually occurred. *Anything they tell me won't alter my views.*

R   You were not present.

M   I was not present.

R   You have of course to take your subordinate's word.

M   The facts speak for themselves. The men threw down their tools and went out without giving their legal week's notice.

R   Oh, we know they didn't give notice. We have guessed this would happen sometime if the grievance went on.

M.   They have gone out on this point - a man of your society, a journeyman, has been objected to for putting in ½ in. rivets, not a 'knobstick', not a boy, an apprentice who has served his time to the trade and a member of your Society.

R   That is just why I should like you to see the men. Their tale is quite different to that.

M   Perhaps I may have the men in when we come to some conclusion with you as the representative of the Society.

The arguments then ranged round the run down of the seven to eight squads of full paid journeymen in the shop to one, that a journeyman of 30s. per week was being replaced by a 24s. per man. It was the issue of using cheaper labour and cutting the wage bill that was 'the straw that broke the camel's back' riposted Richards, 'They have had so many of these grievances lately. A shop should not be upset this way.' Marsh retorted,'The upsets are of their own making'.

R   A difference of opinion then.

Marsh then proceeded to use one of his bees in his bonnet. 'You don't want to tell me that men, because they are employed in the Brighton Works, are of a different class to anybody else, are to be treated differently.'

R   Certainly not; I say that they should have been treated in the manner in which they are used to be treated.
M   If you don't want to accept any principle that the men here are to be treated differently to members of your Society in other districts in England, we shall get on all right, but if you want to accept that principle, I must say 'Goodbye'.
R   We do not want these 'reforms' as you call them, introduced into the place. You choose a place where these 'reforms' are worse for the men than any other place in the kingdom. I should like to see matters settled somehow or other, or it is likely the dissatisfaction will spread'.

He went on to speak of 'great dissatisfaction and threats to put those young fellows on, and by and by you would do without them altogether'.
    The controversy then moved on to riveting, Marsh throwing out, 'A member of your Society said "Look here, you are not to put in more than 40 a day"'.

R   Who told you that?
M   It is not right to tell.

R   They tell me that task work is practically introduced here, and men are expected to put in 150 rivets a day or something like that.

Here Bennett interrupted saying 'That is what I consider a satisfactory day's work, 100-150'.

M   And they want to limit a pneumatic long stroke hammer to 40! I have instanced these one or two cases to show the unreasonableness of the men.

R   I should like of course the men to hear these statements, because some of them are conflicting.
M   One tale is always good until you hear the other. There is bound to be dissatisfaction when you come to a place where for many years the men have been the masters.

Marsh was not prepared to accept Richard's contention 'that the men are dissatisfied because the old order of things in the shops has not been allowed to remain'. 'I am afraid from what you say; I shall not sign these boiler orders (for construction at Brighton works). They will have to be done somewhere else', he threatened.
    There followed a heated exchange when Richards, viewing past practice in the boiler shop said, 'I do not think that they had low priced men working with high priced men'. Bennett interposed. 'How are you going to learn your apprentices if you are not going to allow them to knock down a ½ in. rivet?' Marsh replied, 'I think you will admit the best was done under the circumstances'.

R   Not so, a small matter has triggered off a general dissatisfaction.
M   What do they want?

R   They want their grievances be redressed [complaining of Bennett threatening to put boys on men's work]. They have always been noted for good work here and have taken their time for it. They have to work harder now and do not mind but they look at it in another light. They are put on task work practically and sweated. You can go too far with the men.
M   We expect much harder work than they have done in the past.

R   There is nothing wrong about that, but you expect them to take their shirts off.

Bennett intervened; 'One fellow in particular in the crowd said "Come, let us bloody well go out"'.

R   Our Society does not encourage anything like that, but I am positive that the men will not come in until they get their grievances settled. The greatest grievance is putting *under priced men on what full time men have been doing.* It is not right.

Marsh then called in the men, a deputation of five including patchers, riveters and holder-ups.

R   Mr Marsh considers a deputation should have been asked to see him before going out. I understand that was asked for and refused, but Mr Marsh says it was not. James Stelfox the boiler shop steward, interjected 'I turned round to the men and said, "Go back to your work and we'll see what we can do", but the men were determined. While they stood there the under manager said, "If you don't go to your work, you had better go out".' The exchange moved on to a point when Marsh exclaimed 'Do you tell me that an alteration had taken place since I have been here, the rate of the men altered?'

The leading workman replied, 'I do not say on the whole, a great deal of it has. I should like to point out the sets have been split up since you have been here'.

M   What other grievances have you?
LW   Continual harassing, - saying we have never done enough when we are working as hard as we can. I do a fair day's work for a fair day's pay.
M   How do you justify a man asleep at work? We have found several men asleep at their work. Matters have been going on too easy lines. This is the reason I got a fresh foreman.

R   That's where the trouble comes in.
M   No doubt, if the men have been having their own way for several years they will object to any alteration.

R   Look here, Mr Marsh. Do you think a man can work with a good heart when he is continuously harassed with 'You are not doing enough. You will have to push on. If you don't, we will have to get someone else'.
M   You can take it from me, it will pay us to get the work done outside if you do not do more than you have done in the past.

About 200 double bolster trucks were built from 1899 onwards. Their loads were by no means restricted to timber. This pair, Nos. 7761 and 4042 are standing in a corner of Brighton works yard loaded with boilers waiting their turn to go into the erecting shop. The photograph is one of several taken by Frank Burtt at the works.

Frames for new locomotives are seen in the foreground. The north end of the erecting shop opened out to the adjacent machine shop providing almost direct access for items to be machined and returned according to the requirements of the fitters.

LW I find that we are working day work harder than we worked piecework.
M   Do you object to piecework?

R   We object on principle.

LW I object to the system.
M   You want a shop where there is no foreman or manager!

Marsh was at a loss: 'I do not see why the men should strike on the matter of this one man. Is there any reason why they did not strike before?'

LW The men have tried to avoid this. They have seen it coming sometime; trouble coming. They have tried to work amicably with all concerned.

This was enough for Marsh: 'Now you are no longer members of the Company, you are all fresh hands if you come in again. You have forfeited your access to pay and you have forfeited your pension - those who belong to it. You know the rules'.

LW We know what is happening in other departments and we don't want it to occur to us. In the paint shop today there are men working 3 days instead of 6, coming up to know if there is any work for them. We believe in a regular week's work.

M   You take exception to our change in the method of painting. You don't know the full story, and are not fitted to judge. The work has been altered in such a way that there are more men than we want for painting, and sooner than discharge them I am painting all the machines instead of sacking them.

Marsh then offered an olive branch, 'I am only empowered to tell you this. I am quite willing to let bygones be bygones if the men will go back on the same terms as they left'.

LW The men are determined not to go back until the full paid man goes back to the same on the tanks. We went to the Foreman three times on the question of this man before coming out.
R   I believe these delegates did their best to keep the men at work.
M   They might have given notice that they objected. You know the rules, to give a week's notice and in lieu of that notice forfeit your arrears.

R   That shows the grievance must have been genuine.
M   It was evidently clearly in a momentary fit of temper.

R   It was a determination of the men. They will not have a low rated man on tank work.
M   Suppose we haven't a full paid man? Are we to stop a boiler?

At that point Alexander interjected: 'As a matter of fact, none of this would have cropped up if your men had kept better times. Absolutely bad timekeeping is one of the biggest bugbears we have to contend with - and not just the boilermakers'.

M   You are a class of men by yourselves. You live in Brighton and have had privileges in the fact which you do not get in any other shop in the kingdom, and mean to keep them. I cannot accept a theory like that; there is no justice in asking for exceptional treatment. A man from Leeds or Manchester is as good as you are. There is a feeling among them that because they are in Brighton they should be treated in an exceptional manner. They had an exceptionally easy time of it.

LW   There has been exceptional work done on the railway; work, never in a railway shop like the Brighton Railway!

Bennett chipped in, I have been told 'You are not at Swindon now, you are in Brighton and must do as Brighton does'.

M   Why should you object to *improvement*?

R   We object to the style of progress; we don't think it a reform.

M   No doubt we shall never see eye to eye on this matter. You are bound to find disaffection in a shop run by itself for years. The foreman has not authority over you.

LW   Yes, he certainly had.

M   Well, not to my satisfaction.

LW   We know a Foreman is not a very enviable position, but you are entitled to civility whether in Brighton or anywhere else.

M   It is all in your interests. If we do not get the work done by men efficiently at Brighton, we shall get it somewhere else. Mr Alexander has brought in these orders for 20 boilers and for 50 steel underframes, all with one view, to get them cheaper than we do here. If not, we shall not have them.

Marsh was becoming vindictive and the arguments were getting nowhere. Richards was becoming impatient, 'I think we have had a good discussion on the matter. I should like to know your decision, whether the men, if you decide to let matters go on as usual, can have a full priced man on this particular job, and then discuss the matter of men on steam tight work'.

M   The best advice I can give the men is to go back to work under the conditions they went out, and then send a deputation to see me. I shall be very amenable to discuss conditions with them.

R   They will not return to work under those circumstances.

Four times Marsh repeated his offer and four times Richards answered 'Only if a full paid man is put on the job'. That remained the sticking point.

The workmen were asked to retire and, after a short consultation with Alexander, Marsh recalled them, having come up with a way out of the impasse.

M   I began with negotiations with a representative of your Society. Like most . . . I found him a reasonable man. I get an admission from him that he does not and will not uphold you in any action you may take against the introduction of a pneumatic tool. I am willing to put back affairs to the state of things in which they were before you went out: if you like to go back on Monday morning, I shall work that man with a pneumatic tool to rivet down this work. You do not object to that.

LW   Not at 24s. a week.

M   I shall put a 36s. man and he will nobble them down with a pneumatic tool.

R   Convey your answer to our members. Tonight they will decide themselves, but I
     think they will accept your answer. Do I understand this work has not been done
     previously with a pneumatic machine?

A   No. Any other matter will be a special deputation after the men have been prepared
     to resume work on these conditions.

M   Certainly - but let it be clearly understood what these conditions are - this theory
     that Brighton men are different from boilermakers in any other part of this
     kingdom must be dropped, and that this work and any other class of work shall be
     done with pneumatic tools, if thought necessary by the management.

The second document covers a further meeting with the workmen's
delegation on 29th May, 1905. Marsh said they had taken the right course in
coming to see him and they ought to have done so before holding a meeting,
and letting it go forth to the Directors who would naturally say there was
something wrong here, and because the works were to be carried on
commercial lines, the men were going to kick.

Thomas Manning of the carriage shop said it was not the men who brought
about these changes. Walter Evans (of the fitting shop) spoke of the discharges
of men right and left, of seven men dismissed in his shop (fitting and turning
department). Ernest Lucas of the paint shop said every endeavour was made to
keep the meeting private.

Marsh said that coming here as a fresh superintendent, it would be one of the
last things to consider the dismissal of men, not the first thing; to look upon the
old men as the sheet anchor of the concern in which they worked. There was no
question of removing old men from amongst them, he did not know how the
idea had got into their heads. Stelfox of the boiler shop told of the threat to get
rid of eight old boilermakers. Marsh reckoned that the men had jumped at this
conclusion. In any ordinary commercial concern, if they would not get an
ordinary amount of work out of an ordinary man, they would have to get the
best men they could, in the ripest age of life and let the old men go on the
Societies. Manning said he took this to mean getting rid of the old men.

Marsh assured them that no drastic reforms would be done in the works
without consultation with himself; he had the management of men for the last
20 years and appreciated the services of the old ones as having the brains of the
establishment. Lucas asked that when radical changes were contemplated as
regards the wages of men, they should first be discussed. Marsh said that they
would pass on to the next question which came from Manning, asking that
consideration be given to the fact that Brighton was one of the most expensive
towns in England, quite different to Doncaster, Wolverton or Swindon. He had
worked for the LNW for years and had a beautiful house for 5s. a week. He
could not get one in Brighton for 12s.

Marsh replied that the Directors had purchased land outside Brighton to try
to meet this problem. As to men having an advance, he could not agree. He
wanted to get work done in Brighton rather than outside. As an earnest of what
he said, he had already asked the Directors to build 10 engines here, and he had

The machine shop at Brighton works, with its multitudinous belts and shafting overhead, was a hive of activity. Prominent in this photograph are tender frames, planing machines, coupling rods and cylinder centres being bored. Everything is tightly and carefully stacked with space at a premium.

A posed photograph in the machine shop of a team with their bowler-hatted foreman. An amazing variety of equipment is on view including lathes, boring machines, portable drills served by belt drives. On the left side is part of the extensive trolley line system with one of the trolleys providing suitable seating accommodation. Originally known as 'The Locomotive and Carriage Factory', Brighton works at its peak employed over 2,000 people.

told them he must have more work or shut up the place. They would not keep the work going as a matter of sentiment. They were fortunate to be employed by such a company.

The discussion moved on to working short time, a plea to be allowed to come in on Saturday morning, if only to clean the shop. On the question of piecework, Marsh said that in the course of time, those of the men not working piecework would come and ask for it. Evans was afraid Mr Marsh would be disappointed as to this. Marsh said that they might depend on it the Directors had not sent him there if they wanted the place to go on as it was before, but he should not rush. The place was in a bad state and they knew as well as he did. He pointed to his track record saying he could not have got the Doncaster shops into the state of perfection it was, if he had not the goodwill of the men. He had no more time to spare at present as he had to go to London, but would meet them again if they wished.

The third document in the series was a letter from Stelfox of the boiler shop in June 1905, a written statement of the points touched upon at the interview on Monday last, 29th May.

We disavow on behalf of the men any desire to needlessly cause disturbance on the Works, our object is to promote a feeling of goodwill. The men's alarm was justified by dismissals and threats which were primarily the cause of unrest, culminating in the meeting of 22nd May, strictly confined to railway employees. The Press were excluded, we therefore take no responsibility for accounts in the local press. The mere fact of it becoming known to outsiders was due to the widespread character of unrest which at the time prevailed.

Stelfox went on to state the four key points:

1. Piecework which recently suffered considerable reduction. He was fairly well acquainted with the prices ruling at Doncaster, but it was inadequate to meet the additional cost of living at Brighton.
2. Dismissals, not just the actual 20 that had already taken place, but in constant threats to terminate employment that utterly unnerved the men. Permanent employment has been the chief attraction of the Brighton Railway Works.
3. The position of old servants which had arisen through a statement of the Manager. There was a need for an authoritative statement to allay the alarm.
4. Short time, specially affecting the lower paid men receiving 18s. a week.

The final document in this batch was a transcript of a meeting with workmen's delegates on 9th June, 1905. Present with Marsh were W. Alexander (works manager), James Stelfox (boiler shop), Wm Evans (fitting shop), Thos Manning (carriage shop), Ernest Lucas (paint shop) and Jas Waterhouse (wheel shop).

Mr Marsh said that he had received the letter of the 2nd inst. and wished to know what they wanted; they only seemed to ask him to repeat what he told them the other day. Evans replied he came away from the previous meeting without any definite idea of their position. 'The piecework question - was it in force or not.' Marsh replied he had already told them he was not going to say anything.

The smith's shop at Brighton works *c.* 1905 showing a row of forges up against the side wall. Not far away in the centre of the floor would have been the shop's *piece de resistance*, the big steam hammer known as 'The Iron Man'. As with many photographs taken inside the shops, all too often they lack the presence of the human element, the photographer electing for out of working hours, possibly the weekend.

A backhead plate lies wedged at a convenient angle for work to proceed on cutting out the firehole. Until electrical power was introduced in 1908, this kind of work proved hard graft for the workmen, starting with hand drills, then brute force with chisel and hammer and finally a filing down.

Stelfox stated the men in the boiler shop were dead against the piecework system. This was chiefly at the bottom of all the trouble despite Mr Alexander saying that machinery would be installed and the place brought up to date. Despite this, the men had voted dead against piecework; he chiefly believed they thought the prices could be cut down.

Evans said that it was put to Mr Marsh at their last interview that on any matter regarding wages or working conditions which govern wages, the men ought to be consulted, but Marsh replied that it was like asking the superintendent to vacate his chair and the men to sit in it. The delegates repudiated this. They had no desire to interfere with the management of the works, 'but surely there are two parties to the contract, it cannot be a binding one unless both have some power of settling terms'. Marsh sarcastically asked if this meant that when he proposed to give a man a rise, he was to send for them to say!

Lucas knew of a case in the paint shop where 10s. had been knocked off a coach. Marsh explained that money had been knocked off in cases where the works would stand it because the men did not honestly do their best. One man had been known to be asleep for three hours in a gang. Lucas had better argue this with the man who had his price cut down.

Evans remarked that surely Marsh would not as a consequence victimise the whole of the department. Marsh said at Doncaster he could set rates where men earned 50, 80, and 90 per cent on their wages. His point was that piecework was better for the men than task work. It was better for him to give the men an incentive to help him turn out more work.

Waterhouse complained that as a rule the foreman said 'You have to do this at a price', and they never had in the past the privilege of coming to the manager or the superintendent.

Other instances were cited before Marsh concluded the session saying they might like to take it from him that any new methods introduced would be to the mutual benefit of the company and men themselves.

When Marsh reported on the strike to the Brighton Board on 30th May, he explained the matter in this way. The men had objected to the introduction of a low rated man into a riveting gang. The return to work had been on the understanding that such work shall in the future be done by one man and a holder-up working with pneumatic hammers instead of by a man, apprentice and a holder-up. This assimilated this practice with that prevailing in other works in the country. The company could now use as many pneumatic tools as advisable.

The Case of Riveter Cannon

Almost a year later the Board received a joint letter from the Amalgamated Society of Engineers, the Steam Engine Makers Society, the Boilermakers and Iron Steamship Makers and the General Railway Workers Union, speaking of unrest amongst the locomotive and carriage staff at the shops, the Board saying that they were prepared to receive a deputation via the Heads of Departments. On 13th May, 1907 Marsh received another deputation from the boiler shop.

The whole extended fracas centred round the dismissal of riveter G. Cannon who had received his notice to leave on 8th May. He had just finished a bout of work inside a firebox and had come outside when Marsh himself happened to be walking the floor. He accused him of idling, asked him a series of questions the answers of which did not appear to satisfy him, charged him with insolence and gave him his notice. Cannon was a shy unforthcoming man, but his colleagues who had witnessed the incident held a meeting and agreed to send a deputation from the boiler shop. The proceedings show Marsh at his most prickly and peremptory:

Deputation	We had a meeting on the 9th inst, and Cannon stated his case, and we cannot really think what he had his notice for.
Marsh	What do you want to know?
D	It is the wish of the men to ask you to withdraw his notice, as they think he has been harshly dealt with.
M	Do you question my right to dismiss any man in the shop? . . or my prerogative as an employer of labour to give a man a character he deserves.
D	The man was not idling, he had just finished a spell of work inside a firebox, and had come outside.
M	What has that to do with you? I cannot quite understand what you have come to see me for. I have sacked a man because I deem it to the Company's interest that he should be sacked, the same as I should deal with you if I found any of you talking and keeping other men from their work.

The men went on to explain that when there are two sets working on stays, they are obliged to work single handed; if one set have to work double handed, the other has to stand outside in turn.

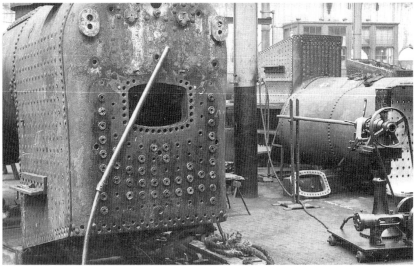

Detail of the boiler shop at Brighton Works. The introduction of electric power for machinery meant that a riveter could do the work in a third of the time it took previously, with the resultant lay-off of employees. The firebox on the left provides a good idea of the work involved, and of riveter Cannon's predicament. Another classic Frank Burtt photograph.

M   That is a question I am not prepared to discuss with you.

D   The man, at the meeting, expressed his opinion that he had not been dealt fairly with, given his notice because he had come out of the firebox. It was only natural and the ordinary way of working, and you asked him what he was doing, and several questions about how they worked at Swindon. And the outcome of it was that he was given notice.

M   Quite right.

D   In answering, Cannon might have said 'no' when he should have said 'yes': he was not well that day. It was some years ago when he worked at Swindon, and he was only a boy then. He did not reply to you in a disrespectful manner, he is not a man of that sort, he is very reserved and has not much to say, and according to his conduct he would not give a disrespectful reply.

M   I have told you what you want to know. Have you any more questions to ask me?

The argument continued, the men pleading Cannon's nervous temperament, Marsh stating that if an appeal was made to the Board of Directors 'I shall be unable to exercise my prerogative of leniency in the future'. Marsh then insinuated that their case was weak. 'I suppose the truth of the matter is this; if you know Cannon was sacked for idling and talking about the shop, you think some of you would be in a ticklish position'. His parting barb to the deputation was 'Well if he (Cannon) thinks you manage the Works instead of me, he was right to come to you. I do not like the tone of your coming to see me. There is something not quite friendly going on in the Works'.

The next morning Mr Richards, delegate from the Boilermaker's Union was at the door.

M   You came about this man, Cannon?

R   Our people ask if you would reconsider your decision for they think the man has been harshly dealt with.

M   Is that all you have come to see me about!

Richards pleaded his case. 'He was not out of the box one minute before you came along when you asked him several questions and he did not know'. But Marsh would not budge.

R   Very good Sir, I have done my duty coming to you and ask you to reconsider the case. It is a serious thing. There is no doubt about it, more than appears on the face of it.

M   Do you mean to tell me they question my prerogative to sack any man? Why do you come here?

R   To ask you to reconsider your decision.

There followed discussion regarding hardship and a blight on any future employment for Cannon, and over the issue of the supposed impertinence. Getting nowhere the experienced Richards now pulled out his trump card, 'I do not think for a moment when this is reported to the meeting at night that it will satisfy the men. I had difficulty in getting them to alter their decision in a resolution they wanted to pass to come out tonight. I believe this time other trades in the Works will come out with them. I am almost positive of it. The men only want a little more to come out'.

M   I expect civility from the men employed, and that they stick to their words. Whether I shall deal leniently or not, is not a matter I shall discuss with you. It is time the nonsense which is going on in the shops is stopped, and the sooner the Directors know about it the better I shall be satisfied.
R   We shall not be able to keep the men back.

M   If my prerogative as Manager of the Works of discharging a man on his misconduct is going to be brought into question, then the sooner I cease to be Manager the better it will be.
R   We understand what you say: if I were in your position I should say the same things.

M   Then why do you come to me?
R   To ask you to reconsider your decision in this particular case. I think it rather harsh, and so do all the men.

M   I am always open to reconsider a case of a man's appeal. He can come along and see me himself if he likes. What I shall do I am not prepared to say. You had better send the man to me if you want that of me.

So later that day riveter Cannon duly appeared to see Marsh.

M   What do you want?
C   I have come to see you about my discharge. I have seen Mr Richards, dinner time. He told me he had seen you, and you reckoned I was rather insolent, but I am sorry if you took me that way. I did not mean it.

M   Why have you not come to me before getting a deputation of your fellow workmen, and then when they do not give you satisfaction, send a delegate from your Society?
C   They took it in their hands.

Marsh sought to imply that Cannon was being used as a tool for the trade unionists, and then turned to the question of insolence, Cannon saying 'I did not know anything about it. I left Swindon 11 years ago, and you asked me the prices there'. At this point Marsh mellowed somewhat, turned to question of circumstances and employment, concluding, 'Well, you have worked out your notice. I will consider the question whether I shall put you on again. I will not promise you, but I will consider it. You can come to me after the Whitsuntide holidays. That is all I can say at present. I must talk over the matter with Mr Alexander (works manager) who is away just now'.

C   I might state we have a meeting tonight, Sir.
M   That has nothing to do with me. You may have what meetings you like. I do not consider that at all.

Cannon got his work back. His case was elbow grease for the boilermakers flexing their Union muscles. The threat of a strike over the issue had caused Marsh to come off his high horse. Having tasted blood, these extreme elements in the works would before not too long be back for more, their unrest further generated by numbers being put on short time. In June 1907 it was noted labourers were working on short time in the Locomotive Department, that 94 men in the shops were working short time earning £1 a week or less, which was affecting their Pension Fund. In May 1908, the General Manager was communicating with Marsh with a view to effecting economies in his department in face of a general increase in expenditure and a decrease in receipts. Marsh agreed to close some of the shops at Brighton from closing time Friday to 6 am the following Tuesday, saving a bill in wages of £1,800 on the proviso that no essential locomotive repairs were delayed to add to those out of repair but leaving him the option to recommence full time in any shop should he consider it necessary.

Enginemen's Deputations

On 18th August, 1908 it was the turn of the locomen to send a deputation of drivers and firemen at Brighton to seek redress of their grievances from Marsh and his running assistant John Richardson. The former had to tread carefully for in these early days of locomotive associations there were rival groups seeking to speak for the men in that occupation. Marsh did his utmost to play them off against each other, opening with 'First of all, tell me whom do you represent?' The Group Secretary, C. Allinson, replied, 'I might say we represent the majority of the men on the Brighton system - the Running men. I can authoritatively say we represent the majority of them'.

Marsh stepped in; 'That is certainly contrary to information I have from the men themselves. You are aware that last year I saw a deputation who represented some 900 men - drivers and firemen'.

A	It includes a very large number of the men we represent today. They are in favour of the views we laid before them in this programme.

The main demand, as so often, was annual increases which Marsh calculated would add £47,000 to the yearly paybill, and went on to add 'The Company are not having such a good time that they are able for a moment to concede such a request'. He then went back to the matter of credentials: 'Do you represent the members of the Associated Society?'

A	We represent members of that Society and a large number who don't belong to either.

M	Why do you not avail yourselves of the Conciliation Board?
A	This is only a preliminary meeting.

Marsh now pulled out his premeditated cudgel with which to deal with this deputation.

I have a letter from the other members, who state they represent the majority of the men - a very reasonable letter - in which they say they recognise the financial state of the Company at the present time, and do not wish any of these demands to be considered for the next 12 months. They hold 900 signatures of engine drivers and firemen to that effect. We have been stopping carriage building, and are getting rid of men, and it is not likely the Company will save money with one hand and spend it with the other. If it came to a Conciliation meeting, the Directors will also have their proposals which might put you in a very much worse position than you are today.

(In this context it is worth noting that following an interview between Marsh and six enginemen in July 1907, the daily rate of pay for drivers with nine years' service was revised up to 7s. 6d. and for firemen with six years' service up to 4s. 6d. This modest increase in wages rewarding experience was to cost the company a mere £1,130.)

The other item was the 8-hour day: 'We are kept almost continuously at work and we feel 8 hours per day is sufficient for the responsibilities we have'. Again Marsh made the financial calculation.

It means £30,000 a year. I can assure you this is not the time to ask such sweeping advances as you are doing here. I may say the Directors are now considering further retrenchments, and I don't think they would for a moment consider these, especially in the face of the letter I received from the other deputation that these matters stand over 12 months . . . Never mind what your ideas are about the hours of labour and the price of labour. Now is not a very opportune time from your point of view to press any demands.

(Marsh was quite correct on this for the Brighton had overstretched and overspent on a series of track quadrupling together with the virtual rebuilding of Brighton works, and had cancelled its plans to quadruple the Brighton line south of Haywards Heath.)

Marsh was quickly back to questioning their credentials, 'Do you represent the countrymen as well as the London men?' and found himself mired on the question of extra costs in living expenses in London where the men were demanding an extra 3s. a week so as to come in line with the other companies, and in the vastly different costs of living in Eastbourne vis-à-vis Horsham.

I advise you not press claims at this present juncture. You could not find a worse time. You do not have such strenuous work as they do on the northern lines. You do not have such hard work when firing and working your engines. This is more or less a tram line as compared with the others. Well I do not know that we can get much further. If you take my advice you will let the matter drop for the time being. You evidently are not representatives of the majority of the men, if I am to attach any importance to this document from the other deputation.

Before he could finish Marsh was asked whether he considered 8 hours a day an unreasonable request. Marsh quoted the 8.45 train from Brighton returning with the 5 pm train only to be reminded by Richardson, 'He takes a train to Wimbledon and back in the meantime'. Marsh then opened the floodgate: 'If you give me any special instance, I am quite willing to consider the cases' and the representatives quickly waded in: 'I was on the main line firing on the

Willesden turn. There is very little opportunity of having a mouthful of food at all'. His colleague quoted an extreme case:

I had the 11.25 down to Worthing a week ago last Saturday. Certainly it was late down, but in every circumstance it is closely timed. We are entitled to get a little food at some time. A man cannot go for 10 hours. On this particular occasion I went on to the table at Worthing 10 minutes past 2 for the 2.20 back to Brighton. I had a quarter of an hour to turn and get back for the 3.35 pm to Portsmouth. Down to Portsmouth at 5.50, out again at 7.5 pm. Half an hour late in, consequently I had not sufficient coal, had to scramble over to Fratton for coal, and I would like to point out to you, Mr Marsh, although we may not have quite the stress of the northern lines, we are mostly kept shunting and almost continually at work.

Marsh stopped this tirade; 'If you will be advised by me, you will go away and drop these matters pro tem. I do not think you there is any possibility of your getting anything. In fact we are getting rid of men here in the shops, and working short time against my wish, but the financial situation embarrasses the Directors so much that it has to be done'.

On 8th February, 1909 it was the turn of the delegation appointed by the Associated Society of Locomotive Engineers and Firemen (ASLEF) to meet Marsh. Credentials were immediately questioned. The Association numbered 645 men on the footplate plus a small number of cleaners. Marsh queried; 'But what about the 900 odd men you said you represented the last time you were here?' 'That included signatures from some of the other Society', came the reply. Marsh explained: 'I have been marking time with Gill and that lot, but it would be a bad thing for you and all the drivers on the line if they go for arbitration. I cannot see what on earth their game is. They must know they have got more benefits than the northern lines'.

Under discussion were the terms of service, whether the delegation represented the majority and of this the Board of Trade (BOT) would need to be convinced, the question of arbitration and of more frequent medical examinations. The latter was a major concern as it related to accidents caused by the mental condition of the men who feared an increase in the number who would be certified as unfit.

'A recommendation by the BOT cannot be lightly brushed aside, you know', Marsh explained. In reply to the question of 'How often?' he surmised 'I have in my mind every five years as a reasonable time'. He was asked what would be the effect on a man's position should he fail to pass the examination. 'Speaking off book somewhat', Marsh responded, 'I should say it would not interfere with their claims on the Pension Fund'.

Marsh then switched to 'How is it the Amalgamated Society complained of the treatment of the men at Battersea?' It brought forth the fact that within the past two years there had been 40 cases of men passing signals at danger. Driver Cooper of Battersea commented, 'That is the fruit of an all grades Society. There is a difference between overshooting and running past if a man tries to stop'. To which Marsh retorted, 'We have had several bad cases, Cooper, not of overrunning one but two or three!' Cooper rejoined: 'As regards the Conciliation Board, we shall do all in our power to upset the other side in going

Another corner of the boiler shop. The boilers display their order numbers, and could be newly ordered examples. This vertical picture shows the overhead gantry manufactured by Craven Bros Ltd of Manchester and delivered in 1895. Boilers were a large and vital component in the manufacture and maintenance of locomotives.

to the Arbitrators', causing Marsh to conclude, 'Judging from the state of trade, this is about the worst time to go to any Arbitrators about the question of any advances'.

At the end of March it was reported that the locomotive superintendent had received petitions for improved conditions of service from the men in his department. Referred to the Board, the proposals were refused and counter proposals laid before the Conciliation Board.

The Strike of 1909

On 9th June, 1909 the Board heard reports of a prevalent strike threat of the boilermakers. Marsh had already discharged 33 men on account of shortage of work. Three had appealed but it was agreed F.J. Avenall alone was entitled to any compensation, but he had declined to resume piecework offered when the system was not universally applied. Avenall together with J. Stelfox and E.J.Taylor alleged they were good workmen but had been discharged because of their trade union connections, having represented their fellows in disputes. The piecework offered could not be accepted unless the piecework system was universally applied. The pressure was rising, for on 19th July the Mayor led a deputation comprising four Aldermen and the Town Clerk from Brighton Corporation stressing that the damage done if there was a strike would amount to a 'calamity'. Despite the plea the boiler shop altercation continued over the issue of the composition of gangs employed in a certain class of riveting work. The Board played for time by directing Marsh to restore the old practice with the proviso that when the shop was in proper working order it would adopt the practice of other companies. In August the Directors saw the three men in question. Avenall read a statement alleging the existence of various grievances and asked for reinstatement and a discussion of the question of piecework. The Board promised to make careful enquiry as regards their individual cases, but the decision could not be altered. If additions were needed to the permanent boilermaking staff, they would be considered.

On 11th October the Board agreed to hold an enquiry upon the three resulting in a memorandum setting forth the whole investigation, but they were too late for early next month, November 1909, 107 men and 61 lads downed tools. Marsh now had a major strike on his hands, the recriminations from which were to sour labour relations irretrievably leaving many long-term employees out of work. Marsh saw this as an opportunity to trim down the workforce while Brighton works was under reconstruction.

Once again it was the militant boilermakers who had come out at 3.15 pm on the 8th over a demarcation dispute. On the 11th Mr Richards was down again to represent the members of his association, complaining that a labourer had been put on the job of cleaning up and chipping a smokebox front. This he considered a boilermaker's work. He was aware that this was formerly done by fitters, but sometime ago it was handed over to the boilermakers. He said that a file was a mechanic's tool, and so were a hammer and chisel. When the work was handed over to the boilermakers and afterwards put into the hands of a labourer, the men objected - and - rightly objected. On the Great Eastern, Metropolitan and Lancashire & Yorkshire Railways, boilermakers did the work in question.

Marsh summoned a bevy of works foremen. One denied such work had been done by the boilermakers since his arrival, conceding only on circular (new) smokeboxes by the boys in the boilershop. Another said it was not new work but repaired smokeboxes that were in question. A third stated that in his time all the finishing off of the fronts of repairs and new smokeboxes had been done in the erecting shop, conceding that there had been only three or four cases in a 12 month when boilermakers had been sent for to chip off some of the metal which had been improperly left on. Marsh agreed to meet the boilermakers' representatives in a week's time.

The 18th November found Marsh in aggressive mood, believing he held the whiphand. 'You have come to open negotiations for restarting? Well now, start the ball rolling then'. The representatives were agreed that the work should not be taken out of the mechanic's hands and placed in the hands of a handyman. A lively argument ensued over demarcation lines, whether new round smokeboxes or repairs, whether it had been done by boilermakers before and when it had been altered, whether boilermakers had been occasionally called into the erecting shop on work that was really a fitter's job.

Marsh cut the discussion short and took up the cudgel.

In plain English it comes to this - Foreman Bennett is not to employ his labourers as he thinks fit. He is not to have jurisdiction in his shop? There are plenty of labourers using hammers and chisels. We have had a lot of talk about these smokeboxes. To get to business, you came to open negotiations in order that you may be re-employed by the Company. If it is not on the basis on your part that work is to be handed to you which has been done by a fitter, we may as well disperse. Is that all you have to say to forward negotiations? You may take this message that they are not going back on the condition that boilermakers are going to be put to do fitters work, and further I shall not recommend the Directors to re-employ any except that under the conditions that the boilershop will be considered an open shop. We are not going to be trammelled in the future as in the past for you men to say who we are going to put on, that you must select the men. It will have to be an open shop and, moreover, any men the Directors may see their way to employ will have to work on piecework. I do not say I am going to make a non-Society shop of it. I say, if you are going to be re-employed, you will have to come back to it as an open shop, and if it is our will and pleasure I may re-employ non-Society men. I am suggesting that this shop shall be run as any other loco shop in the kingdom. If you refuse that, the responsibility is on your own shoulders.

Marsh then drove the knife in deep.

There is no probability of many of you men getting back this year. There will be no new work done here anyhow before Christmas. Work for certain men may be found in the Erecting Shop and Running Shed, but all new work is at a standstill until the beginning of the next year. Machines are being removed in the Boiler Shop and cranes are being pulled down. You have given us a clear hand and I have handed the shop over to the Engineers Department and Mr Allan's fitters. [The death had occurred of Mr Alexander, the works manager, in March 1908 and he had been replaced by Mr A. Allan.]

The representatives responded, 'As our men came out in a body, we don't think it fair for some to come back and others not'. Marsh deflected that issue by stating 'I would go a step further and get the Directors to consider such men as could be employed later on as suspended rather than as no longer in the service, so that they may retain the benefits of the Pension Fund'. The meeting was adjourned until 3 pm on the morrow, again in the Locomotive and Carriage Department, Brighton.

Marsh opened: 'You might tell me what your members say about the two terms I imposed as to your returning to work or not'. The deputation's spokesman replied, 'Well sir, we submitted your proposals to the men yesterday afternoon and they cannot entertain them'.

M Do they take exception to one more than the other. I speak of the question of the Open Shop and of piecework.
D Three conditions really - You said also it is only to be a part of the men who would come back.

M I said we should take back all the men we could. Clearly you understand we should not take back all; we don't want them. For instance in the Running Shed we had 10 to 12 boilermakers, we shall not want these. They are not required.
D As far as the men in the Shop are concerned, we cannot see any reason why the whole of the men cannot go back.

M I explained to you that the machines are all pulled up, the cranes if they are not at present dismantled, will be in the course of next week.
D But they would come back eventually?

M If I had the work for the men we should certainly take those we could, but your delegate said you all wished to come back *en bloc*, and I said it was out of the question altogether.

D It was said that piecework would be brought about in the near future, or a different system would be introduced.

M Piecework and general adoption of modern methods.
D As far as the open shop is concerned, that is absolutely out of question. Our Society would not allow us to do that.

M But do you admit that open shops are the order of the day in all railway boiler shops?
D We do not admit that. A Society and non-Society man do not work together.

M It would not matter to me in this place whether a man was Society or not so long as he did his work.
D These things have always a tendency to cause friction among men.

M But now that you are not in the Company's service, it is natural that the management, in restarting a Shop would want to do so on the same lines as other railways.

Lifting a boiler was always a delicate operation. Here a 'B4' boiler is held by just a single chain attached at the point of balance, requiring the full concentration of the staff concerned. Other work goes on in the background.

Frank Burtt's sharp photograph shows the boiler yard at Brighton with new or renovated boilers standing outside the doors of the boiler shop. Used boilers for disposal would not have blocked up such a vital thoroughfare in the works. In the background wooden scaffolding indicates the picture was taken at the time of the expansion of the works, and also that over the rebuilding period boilers might have been brought in from firms like the Yorkshire Engine Co.

Eventually the representatives gained the concession that all of the men would be considered as only suspended for the time being, only for one them to chirp up, 'Mr Marsh says that some of us have to go', to which Marsh replied, 'For what I can see of the future of Brighton Railway and Brighton Works, there is not room for all of you to come back. Do not take it as an *ipse dixit* that you are all coming back. We should find work for as many men as we can, if you come back. We have work for frame patchers and for hand riveters, and there is work in most of the shop except on new work'.

The final crunch meeting took place on 30th November at 9.30 am in the locomotive and carriage engineer's offices, with the fullest array of delegates present including Mr Allan, works manager, Messrs Richards and Ratcliffe from the Boilermakers Union and five representatives from the workforce. Marsh opened, 'I was asked to meet you today by the delegates of your Society [whom he had met on the 27th]. The principal reason why I have done so is that you have played one against the other, and therefore agreed to see you both together'.

Marsh took a hard line:

Soon after I had been in office here, some men threw down their tools, on a paltry excuse and, after being out for two or three days, were reinstated on the understanding that the Boiler Shop should be carried on in the same manner as on other railways. Events however, falsified this, and led me now to impose the conditions which are *sine qua non* if any men restart in this factory.

Ratcliffe replied:

I had been in hopes the Superintendent would see his way to remove that restriction and, if he would do that this morning, I am quite satisfied he can take this assurance from the delegates of the Society that we will prevent similar stoppages of work in the future, agreeably to the Employers' Liability Societies throughout the country.

M   I do not know of any Employers' Association connected with the Railways at all. [There was an argument over the joining of Societies, Marsh emphasising membership was not obligatory.]

R   In view of the fact that in the Brighton shops for 60 years we have had Society men, and that we have made one or two mistakes, it seems to me however that these mistakes have not been all on one side.

M   The men have not been free members. The younger bloods in the Society have forced the others into it. There was too much Socialism about. Are you going in the right direction to get public opinion on your side when you have three of your workmen who say they will break their fellow workmen's heads unless they come out on strike? Since I have been in office here I have had the same complaint from my Works manager, Mr Alexander, Mr Field and now from Mr Allan. It is the men.

R   I regret such a statement.
M   It is absolutely plain fact.

R   I submit that in the general interests of the town, with the Season coming on, that a dispute of this description makes it worse. I submit that you have men capable of conferring with the Management of your Shops. That is all we are asking for - via a Committee of the men.

M   What different treatment are you getting? I am receiving deputations almost every day. If I have to put a man on from Doncaster, or will we say 'Jericho' (as the word 'Doncaster' does not seem to be appreciated), I am to have a Committee from the men to ask if I am to start him. Before there is going to be any peace in the Works, this state of things will have to be uprooted to get back to an open shop and freedom of employment.

R   I expect something more from you, Mr Marsh . . .

A purple and revealing passage indeed! A hard fought compromise was thrashed out. The men were not to forfeit their three days pay whilst on strike; but there was acrimony over the rate. Ratcliffe asked Marsh to pay the rate adopted by the Society to which the latter retorted, 'I will pay a man what I think he is worth?' Then Marsh quoted several cases of intimidation, but eventually gravitated back to thrashing out a compromise on the redundancy issue. Allan suggested taking back 50 men, Marsh cut it down to 20 with an undertaking to sign on 60 per cent of the men who went out when the shop was running again. 'Not being inconsiderate, I will give you this pledge: We will not swamp you out with non-Union men. I advise you, however, if I were you, swallow the question of the open shop'. The parties concerned agreed to meet in two days time.

On 2nd December Marsh opened: 'Well now, have you any news for me?' Ratcliffe came up with an alternative set of proposals:

1. The first is that Mr Marsh has the liberty of employing who he likes; we reserve to ourselves the right to make any eligible boilermaker a member of our Society.
2. That we entertain piecework on the conditions laid down by the Directors in their memorandum, that the men shall be consulted with regard to the value of their labour.
3. That the members are not anxious to commence work in the Brighton Shop until such time as the shops are ready for them to work in.

M   I do not quite understand the last suggestion.

Ratcliffe reminded him that he had said he wanted 20 men, and that this would lead to dissension if a certain few were started while the remainder were kept waiting until the shops were ready. Marsh returned to the subject of coercion of men to join the Society and the question of stoppages.

Ratcliffe responded: 'Now, Mr Marsh, will a simple addendum satisfy you that no stoppage of work shall take place until such time as you and the representatives of the Society have had an opportunity of considering and advising the men'. Marsh was not wearing that; 'That is merely putting your own men back today with all probability of having them out again this day week. With regard to the last amendment I do not think we can fall into that'. It was suggested re-employing the 20 men in relays so as to give all a turn, and this was taken away for the management to talk over.

The final round of this extended saga took place on New Year's Eve 1909, called as a result of a telegram sent to Marsh. Since the previous meeting the Mayor of Brighton, concerned for the welfare of the town, had intervened as an intermediary, interviewed Marsh, discussed proposals for the resumption of work and set Monday 3rd January as the date the shops would reopen. The sticking point was Marsh's willingness to see a deputation from the men. Marsh confirmed that he had seen the Mayor, but nothing would be done till the Works were opened. Nothing was said about receiving a deputation of the men. The Boilermakers Society had taken exception to Mr Allan sending for 16 men and telling them they could resume work. The men had refused to accept the offer, the Society having advised them not to resume work, the matter having been decided by a majority of the whole of the men at a meeting which was called. The question was whether Marsh was prepared to modify the conditions already laid down. He replied: 'Same offer as before. Besides the members of the Society in the Works had been the most unsatisfactory members of any society he had ever come across in his life. The proceedings up to the present did not fill him with any good hopes for the future. There seems to be some sort of breach of arrangement between them'.

Marsh said that if they wanted to get their men jobs in other parts of the country, they would do well to get them to alter their tone. He was told of a workman the other day who said he was a good workman who liked to take his time over a job! Ratcliffe asked how long it would be after the 20 men started before the rest of the men were required. They had been out eight weeks, and there must be lots of work. Marsh replied that they were never in a better state. He happened to have 100 spare engines about the line. Allan suggested taking on a few men each week as the shop being was set out. Marsh had the last word by promising to do what was possible to get the shop ready in a fortnight's time.

On 5th January, 1910 Marsh reported on his interview to the Board. He had said men could return if they accepted the open shop and piecework system, a demand which he knew would divide the opposition. Sure enough, 21 men returned as 'temporary hands.' Marsh was authorised to restore them and others who returned to 'permanent' staff on accepting the conditions and assuring them their pension rights were safeguarded. At the start of February another 20 were received back. But a month later a petition from 11 boilermakers ('whom it is proposed not to re-employ') asking for re-employment in consideration of their long service, was declined. Similarly an enginemen's deputation pleading for an additional increase in wages for drivers of motor trains on behalf of the extra work involved was turned down without any offer being made.

All this left the company under attack from a discontented labour force. There had in Marsh's final year been a threatened strike at Brighton works over the allocation of work. These rumblings contributed to a full railway strike on 18th August, 1911 which led to a direct loss in passenger receipts of around £20,000.* It had commenced over difficulties with staff at Willow Walk arising out of the unsettled conditions of labourers in the transport trades then existing in London and elsewhere which resulted in over 400 men comprising carmen, checkers, members of the platform staff and others ceasing work and thereby causing considerable dislocation and delay to goods traffic, and then spread to drivers, firemen and cleaners in the Metropolitan area. Worse was to come with a coal and docks strike called on 1st March, 1912 which lasted until Easter and restricted services for eight weeks.

* This was part of a 2 day National Railway Strike.

There are no further meetings recorded during Marsh's superintendency. Inevitably relations between management and unions ended in compromises out of which there were no clear winners. The battle lines became more hardened and, as unions pushed for more definition, the grey areas in dispute became set in stone. Marsh and the boilermakers each gave as good as they got but each gain was balanced by an equal concession. The strike was a telling weapon, damaging the company, only to be tempered by the latter's lack of finance and threats of redundancy. Marsh fought his corner aggressively but had lost the goodwill of the workforce the day he arrived.

A Lesson in Man-management

How different to the approach of Lawson Billinton who, having worked on the Brighton shopfloor under his father, sought to take into account the feelings of the men and to understand their situation. Very early on at the start of his superintendence on 21st August, 1911 he met a Deputation of Brighton drivers and firemen to discuss their grievances. This was held against the background of a national strike. The locomotive men at Brighton had held a meeting two days earlier at which 80 men present had decided to be loyal and not strike. They represented both the Societies and non-Society men and elected eight delegates to see Billinton and enumerate their grievances. It is worth looking at these briefly, bearing in mind Marsh had gone over much of this ground during his regime, but solved very little.

There were eight issues listed for attention, but opportunity was given to discuss additional items not on the agenda. Those covered included firemen on the main line not receiving main line pay, 9 hour Sunday turns, short stayovers in London insufficient to prepare locomotives, an extra quarter-hour for firemen to book on, limits of loads for goods trains, meal times for crane drivers, mess rooms for enginemen, 'All Stations' passes for enginemen, eyesight tests, meal breaks for relief men and insufficient oil allowance. All received a sympathetic answer and assurance to look into them further.

Lawson Billinton concluded the meeting with these words. 'I take it as a personal compliment to myself that the Brighton men behaved as they did', words that would never in the wildest imagination have surfaced in Marsh's vocabulary. He was referring to Brighton enginemen amongst others who had held back in the 'Great Railway Strike' that brought to a head a period of poor industrial relations. This had ended on 19th August, 1911 upon the promise of setting up of a Royal Commission. Indeed, that October the local press reported that 'railwaymen were called into the waiting room at Brighton Station to be thanked officially for not striking'. Even a grateful public, relieved that their daily commuting had not been interrupted, patronised a 'Thanks' fund raised by public subscription, the major payment being £ 94 16s. 6d. to 'Central Traffic and Platelayers'.

Chapter Six

Indiscretions

Bearing in mind Marsh's shortcomings in both character and relationships, especially with the workforce, and the resulting unpopularity, it should have come as a surprise that rumour, prattle and innuendo rampaged through the company's employees and in particular on the shopfloor. Due to an unfortunate set of circumstances, tongues in Brighton works began to wag.

The talk was of a 'ghost' Atlantic, No. 36, and that Marsh had sold away the parts of this missing engine. The true facts are these that five Atlantics with tenders were ordered from Kitsons by Marsh in April 1905, shortly after taking office. The price at first was £3,950 each, later reduced by £45 when Marsh wrote requesting delivery in grey instead of Stroudley yellow. They were all delivered during the winter of 1905-6, and allocated the numbers 37 to 41. Later, in 1910, the last 'I4', No. 35, having been completed the previous year, those in the erecting shop discovered sets of motion parts stamped '36'. These in fact belonged to a new design for a 4-6-2 tank whose drawings had been completed in January. The number 36 had been allotted when assembly commenced, being the next vacant number in the general list after the 'I4s', and was originally classified as 'I5' in the Locomotive Register. It was soon altered to 100 (starting a series later used by Lawson Billinton's 'E2' class), before finally settling on 325 which, being the number of Stroudley's famous 'Single' *Abergavenny*, scrapped in 1907, the Board chose to perpetuate the name on the new engine. This move away from 36 was totally logical, for the original authorisation was for six such 4-6-2Ts, the number 37 to 41 being already carried by the first batch of Atlantics. However the damage had been done.

The trouble was that there was a widespread supposition by both railwaymen and enthusiasts that the first of the Atlantics should have been No. 36. Even such a Brighton authority as A.B. Macleod had firmly believed that the first Atlantic should have been No. 36. Philip Evetts, who later worked at Brighton works, recalls:

> My betters were telling me that there were 12 Atlantics, but my school friends said 11. At school in 1925 I received as a prize The *Book of the Locomotive* by G.C. Jackson, which stated on page 180 that there were 12! Accordingly I broached the subject with a man who worked in Brighton Works. He said, 'There should have been 12, but Marsh owned a laundry in Hove which needed a new boiler, so Kitsons "obliged"!' The engine would have been No. 36 and that is why D.E. Marsh was sacked. Philip adds: 'If this is a vicious story, then I must apologise to any descendants of the Marsh family, but recount it as told me in about 1926'.

Bill Coney, an old Brighton driver, understood that the Directors had approved an order for six 'B5' class engines (later known ask 'H1') from Kitsons, while the late Derek Brough recalled that around 1925 there was at East

The mysterious No. 36, the number allotted when assembly of Marsh's new 4-6-2 tank engine began in 1910. This led to rampant rumours of a missing Atlantic whose boiler Marsh was supposed to have sold to a local steam laundry. The virtually complete 'J' tank, later to be No. 325, nears outshopping in Brighton works. Note the 'F' on the chimney denoting 'Front'.

Croydon Signal School a model 4-4-2 running with the number 36. Driver George Washington, who was *Gladstone's* fireman, also believed at the time that Atlantic No. 36 was never constructed but that the boiler was used for a laundry in Hove which Marsh was supposed to have owned. Bill Coney's version was that the laundry needed a new boiler so Kitsons were 'persuaded' to supply and 'forget' to make Atlantic No. 36. If, and there is some foundation for this, Marsh disposed of a boiler to the Brighton and Hove Steam Laundry, why supply a huge, powerful, brand new Atlantic boiler when there were so many surplus boilers lying around Brighton works yard? Hearsay, driven forward by a whispering campaign, had put two and two together, but add up they did not.

These on the surface were outrageous rumours which, though unfounded, unfortunately stuck, being, as C. Hamilton Ellis relates in his *The London, Brighton and South Coast Railway*, taken up 'by the Sunday gutter newspapers, about a missing locomotive which, it was alleged, Marsh had never built, although by some means or other he was supposed to have pocketed the money'.

Financial Dealings

'Filthy lucre' appears to have been Marsh's undoing. Why this desperate need to fill his empty pockets will probably never be known. Philip Evetts asks, 'Where did he blow his money - on fast women or slow horses?' Was he involved in failed schemes and failing businesses? In the lingo of the day, the refined Edwardians would have described him as a 'a bounder'. But whatever, is it possible that he was in constant debt, and that this grew to such proportions that he succumbed to selling second-hand railway materials on the side and pocketing the proceeds?

A concrete example of his inability to pay his debts is provided by an item from Dick Riley's collection. A bill from the Metropole Hotel, Brighton, shows that even in very small financial matters Marsh was known to be tardy in payment and clever in deferring the moment of payment. He regularly frequented this grand establishment as befitted a person of his high status and appears to have received a 25 per cent discount as a regular patron. He may have taken a business colleague or possibly his wife for a luncheon which concluded with liqueurs. The bill on 10th December, 1906 came to 10 shillings in total with a 3*d.* tip for Waiter No. 2. Paid it was, but, as Dick Riley aptly comments, 'It has been torn in half to prevent him from sending it again to the LB&SCR Co.'s Locomotive Department account'.

Certainly something of Marsh's financial opportunism was handed down to the next generation. Philip Evetts was at Swindon in the early 1930s at the same time as John (Jack) Marsh who was two years his senior.

> He struck me as a man who had little interest in railways, and was looked upon as a 'wide boy' by some Swindon people. I shared the same landlady who found he was slow in paying his rent and recall how John Marsh's room was full of small tea packets. He had fallen for a scheme to make money in his spare time. He would buy two tea chests and had packeted small amounts hoping to sell them off at a 200 per cent profit,

3 Chichester
Place
1/9/11

Dear Mr Payne
As you have
had the matter of
these monies in
hand for me I
wish you would see
the job through.
I will let you have
any further cash
you may want
I am afraid the job
will get muddled if
I take it on in the
middle & there is not

much more to come.
get the food folk
to knock off all
the Railway carriage
charges.

Yours sincerely
D Earle Marsh

Wilson & Smith
are builders & architects
I have to pay!

Above: Letter written by Marsh regarding various financial matters, and hinting certain invoices remained to be paid.
R.C. Riley Collection

Right: Bill from the Hotel Metropole, Brighton, torn in half to prevent Marsh from claiming a second time on the company's expenses account. *R.C. Riley Collection*

2278
Waiter's No. 2
Chance 2 3s 'c RCe Ltd

.. Metropole, Brighton. ..

Breakfasts		8
2 Luncheons		
Dinners		3

1 - 4 st
Leg

HOTEL METROPOLE PAID BRIGHTON

Attendance

Dec 25/6

Total

going door to door. Most of the tea was spilt in his bedroom and very few packets were sold. The scheme failed miserably. To be fair, although he was always short of money we heard of no scandal, but he had a record of debt like his father. He didn't stay on the railway, but disappeared into thin air. At the 1947 reunion of Swindon men no one had heard anything about him since he left the Works.

Defamatory Libel

The saga of disasters was not yet over for Marsh, for he became engulfed in a lurid libel case at the start of 1913. In this matter Marsh was completely exonerated, but the libellous allegations made were unfortunately a reflection of what the general public, encouraged by the media, were thinking at the time.

The case concerned Robert Leaman, 60, a clerk in holy orders who, reading a newspaper report of the 1910 Stoat's Nest rail disaster, noted the mention of Marsh's name. He had known Marsh in Norfolk over 40 years previously. Leaman proceeded to write to Marsh, and subsequently called upon him at his residence at 3 Chichester Place, Brighton. Marsh was very kind to him and Leaman pleading that he had 'fallen on bad times', Marsh on several occasions gave him money, once a guinea and other small sums later, but eventually he told Leaman that he could not help him any more.

Leaman then began writing a series of libellous letters. One of these is quoted in *The Times* law reports for 6th February, 1913, reproduced overleaf:

I know that I am adopting an unusual course in writing to you, but I would have you to consider how basely you have treated me (returning evil for good), not content with being a bad man yourself, in many respects, the gigantic and dishonest way in which you amassed a huge sum of money during the six years you were engineer to the London, Brighton and South Coast carriage works . . . The whole diabolical and co-operative robbing of the shareholders will be exposed, as well as the sweating system of the men organised by you in your department and in every other department . . . As a criminal you will have to forfeit the pension of £500 a year. Mr Lloyd George has full particulars of the bogus balance sheet presented at the general meeting of August 1911, and I feel sure will take up the case, and the Government will brief counsel and fight the case on my behalf, and the world will know that it is wholesale dishonesty and sweating which has caused the great unrest in the world.

As far as the balance sheet was concerned, it was quite innocuous. It all looked very much like a veiled threat of blackmail, once Marsh had declined to assist him any more. Leaman had written a series of accusatory letters, first to Marsh on 7th November, 1912, then to Brewer (Secretary to the LB&SCR) on 9th January, 1913, and also to Lord Bessborough, the Brighton company's Chairman.

Nemesis was close at hand and swift. *The Brighton* Gazette of 1st February, 1913 reported committal proceedings at Tower Bridge Police Court on 29th January. He was charged on warrant 'with unlawfully and maliciously publishing a false and defamatory libel of and concerning D.E. Marsh, knowing the same to be false'. In the hearing of 23rd January he had been unrepresented and the court adjourned . He made a second court appearance on 29th January

Clergyman Sentenced for Libel.

Before the Common Serjeant, ROBERT LEAMON, 60, on bail, a clerk in holy orders, pleaded "Guilty" to publishing a false and defamatory libel concerning Mr. Douglas Earle Marsh, formerly chief mechanical engineer to the London, Brighton, and South Coast Railway Company.

Mr. CURTIS BENNETT, prosecuting, stated that Mr. Marsh had frequently befriended the accused, and eventually told him he could not assist him any more. The defendant then began writing libellous letters concerning the prosecutor, for which there was no foundation. In one of the letters Leamon wrote :— " I know I am adopting an unusual course in writing to you, but I would have you to consider how basely you have treated me, and how ungratefully you have treated me (returning evil for good), not content with being a bad man yourself, in many respects, notably, the gigantic and dishonest way in which you amassed a huge sum of money during the six years you were engineer to the London, Brighton, and South Coast carriage works. . . . The whole diabolical and co-operative robbing of the shareholders will be exposed, as well as the sweating system of the men organized by you in your department and every other department. . . . As a criminal you will have to forfeit this pension of £500 a year. Mr. Lloyd George has full particulars of the bogus balance-sheet presented at the general meeting of August, 1911, and I feel sure will take up the case, and the Government will brief counsel and fight the case on my behalf, and the world will know that it is wholesale dishonesty and sweating which has caused the great unrest in the world."

Mr. W. W. GRANTHAM said the prisoner desired to present an abject apology to Mr. Marsh. The prisoner was suffering from disease, and was not in a normal state of mind when he wrote the letters.

The COMMON SERJEANT said that the prisoner was suffering physically was clear, and therefore the Court could not pass a sentence of hard labour. Leamon would be sentenced to three months' imprisonment in the second division.

The article in the 'Law Reports' section of *The Times* for 6th February, 1913 on the Robert Leaman case.
Courtesy Nick Wellings

when the Magistrate decided there was a case to answer. It was referred to the Central Criminal Court for making 'serious allegations against Mr Marsh'. Bail was set at £50. The result was published in several papers on 6th February including the *Sussex Daily News* which headlined 'Libel on Mr Earle Marsh - Clergyman sentenced' read, 'Yesterday a curious charge of libel came before the Common Serjeant, Sir Alfred Bosanquet KC, at the Central Criminal Court when Robert Leaman, 60, clerk in holy orders, giving an address in Frederick Street, Grays Inn Road, pleaded guilty to an indictment charging him with publishing a defamatory libel of and concerning Mr Douglas Earle Marsh'.

Mr Curtis Bennett led the prosecution explaining the circumstances surrounding the relationship between the two parties which had resulted in proceedings having to be taken to put a stop to 'the interminable nuisance'. Mr William W. Grantham, defending said the prisoner desired to present an abject apology to Mr Marsh. The prisoner was suffering from disease, and was not in a normal state of mind when he wrote the letters. The Common Serjeant said it was clear that the prisoner was suffering physically, and therefore the Court could not pass a sentence of hard labour. Leaman would be sentenced to three months' imprisonment in the second division. This was confirmed in the *Brighton Gazette* for 8th February: 'Prison for Clergyman'. Obviously the whole matter of what he had read in the papers had preyed upon Leaman's mind, but again it was a case of no fire without smoke. Leaman had definitely and outrageously overstepped the mark in expressing openly what others might merely be surmising. No doubt at all, Marsh was deeply hurt by this way-over-the-top defamatory broadside, but the anecdotal evidence suggests that he did sell second-hand materials of the railway company and pocketed the proceeds.

Irregularities

What was the nature of those 'second-hand materials?' Most of the gossip and hearsay centred around the matter of a missing boiler. It is interesting that a query seems to have arisen at the end of the Marsh regime as to the precise number of the 'I2' boilers built and for what purpose. Many were built at Brighton but several were constructed by outside contractors like the North British Locomotive Company, and the 'I2' pattern was used on the 'D3x' and 'E4x' rebuilds and Lawson Billinton's later 'E2s'. There was an adequate float of spares for exchange when in shops and one spare boiler built at Brighton in November 1910 for some reason lay unused until March 1915 when it was sent to Lancing works for temporary use in a stationary capacity!

The late H.M. Madgwick, worked in the clerical corridors of the LB&SCR's immediate successor, the Southern Railway. He had a key job on the freight side as a number taker travelling all over the system chasing up wagons for demurrage, a charge payable on railway trucks that had failed to be loaded or unloaded within a time allowed. Once when discussing this issue he raised the question to the effect, 'When is a perk not a perk?' Certainly nothing has yet been found in any archive of Marsh's employment document defining the parameter of what was a permissible perk or not, but one thing is clear, namely that he grossly over stepped the borderline. Boilers were sold on an official basis to laundries, for example two Billinton type boilers of steel in two rings with the dome on the rearmost, delivered in a batch of five in 1905, were sold in November 1913 to the Sandrock and to the Dexter Steam Laundries respectively, at £605 each, having originally cost £741. However, anything in the nature or otherwise and, worse still, the pocketing of the proceeds, falls completely outside any such contract.

A check through the Finance Committee Minutes on 'Stores Matters', chaired by Charles Macrae with the storekeeper submitting his reports during the later period of Marsh's superintendence, mentions:

> 24th June, 1908 - Disposal of 17 old loco boilers for £1,271, subject to the Locomotive Engineer being satisfied that he cannot get better prices for them if they be broken up.
> 18th May, 1910 - 4 old loco boilers without tubes sold for £258. Loco with tubes £150 after *consultation with the Locomotive Engineer* to J. Livingston & Sons
> 22nd February, 1911 - 3 old boilers for £75 to Cohen & Sons.
> 2nd March, 1911 - 2 old engines for £497 to Messrs Isaacs.

Of possible significance is a Subsidiary Minute of the 16th November, 1910, very close to the time when Marsh began to seek medical treatment, where the Finance Committee, having read the report of the storekeeper made in obedience to a previous minute, referred it back to the storekeeper for further consideration after consultation with the General Manager and the locomotive engineer. On 26th April, 1911 another minute instructed the General Manager, not the locomotive engineer, to advise when old material should be sold, in order to regulate the sales advantageously to the market.

If Marsh had done business on the side, it had unsurprisingly not gone through the books, and the Minutes sound no alarm and mention no missing items or raise any enquiries. In the records of the Locomotive Department's expenditure an entry for June 1911 reads: 'Old material sold'. No details are given, but one is left to wonder whether this might be a write-off covering items that had 'disappeared' from the Works Yard.

The late Donald Bradley at the end of his piece on Douglas Earle Marsh in his *Locomotives of the LB&SCR Part 3* relates how 'when a number of minor irregularities concerning the disposal of scrap material were exposed, the Directors were pleased to accept his resignation when offered on 19th July, 1911'. Bradley had access to company documents and records relating to Brighton works that have long since disappeared, possibly dumped at the time Brighton works were cleared before demolition. Whatever the truth, they failed to reach their true resting place in the National Archives. Perhaps it is fitting that these have not surfaced to add to this sorry saga, but there are sufficient attested facts to account as to why Marsh left Brighton under a cloud. In a personal conversation with Donald at his house in Southborough in 1966, he confirmed that he had seen actual correspondence of the Brighton Board which more or less imported, 'You either retire or we demand your resignation'. There let this overblown episode rest.

Chapter Seven

Indisposition

'Annus Horribilis'

At the 132nd Ordinary meeting of the LB&SCR's shareholders, held at London Bridge in January 1912, the Chairman, the Earl of Bessborough, referred to 'the exceptionally trying year through which we have passed', and alluded to certain circumstances which 'had a distinctly prejudicial effect on the Company's business'.

The year 1911 proved without doubt to be an ill-fated one for the company. There was a backwash of costly compensation payments including two major counts. The first was the so called Stoat's Nest disaster of 29th January, 1910 when, with Marsh Atlantic No. 41 heading the 3.40 pm Brighton-Victoria Pullman express, the last six vehicles came off the rails. The driver, J. Tompsett, finding he could not keep up his brake pressure looked back and saw that his train had divided, the rear part swinging broadside across the track until Marsh elliptical-roofed bogie third No. 1325 crashed violently into the platform ramp blocking all four roads, striking a water column and turning over without its bogies. It contained 71 passengers, five of them were killed instantly together with two unfortunate men standing on the platform. Marsh himself had to give evidence at the subsequent Board of Trade inquiry, stating that the wheel of the leading bogie of No. 1325 had been out of gauge, having shifted an inch on the axle while running and 'must have been subjected to tremendous shock' caused by a long check rail and the bogie mounting the rail. The other disaster was a collision in the Channel between the railway company's Newhaven-based turbine steamship, the fourth to be named *Brighton,* and the sailing ship *Preussen* resulting in a bill of £4,400.

The company, as has been seen, had also been under attack from a discontented labour force. There had in Marsh's final year been a threatened strike at Brighton works over the allocation of work, contributing to a full railway strike on 18th August, 1911.

There was also a locomotive crisis. At the Brighton Board's meeting on 1st February, 1911, the General Manager, William Forbes, submitted 'an investigation requested of certain recent failures of engines'. It revealed that out of 535 locomotives, 155 or 29 per cent were now under repair in the shops at Brighton, Battersea and New Cross and that 118 others, including main line engines, were waiting to pass through the shops. A change in the form of tyres used was blamed as producing a considerable increase of the repair work. It was resolved that 'the Locomotive Engineer be instructed to proceed with 273 engines which were to be in good order by 15th May in time for the summer traffic'. A committee with the Earl of Bessborough as chairman and Charles Macrae as his deputy was instructed to enquire into and report upon the causes for the engine stock being in its present condition and what further steps should be taken.

Health Concerns

What was very apparent, misdemeanours or no, was that the locomotive superintendent was not on top of his job. That Marsh was suffering considerable stress verging on a breakdown is not in question. The imposed strain exacerbated his physical condition and roundabout 1910 he developed a stomach complaint and sought medical treatment. His condition worsened and he was granted an extended period of sick leave. On 15th February, 1911 the Board had been informed by its medical officer, Dr Mitchell Bruce, that the locomotive engineer's state of health necessitated him ceasing work for some time.

What exactly was the nature of Marsh's ill health we are not told, but it was no doubt caused by the tremendous stress bearing down on him from every side. The sad condition of the Locomotive Department coupled with the poor performance of some of his newly-introduced classes, especially the early 'I' tanks, strained labour relations. The suppressed animosity he had to face down, the tangible unpopularity and the constant circulation of rumours and aspersions, would have brought any man to the end of his tether. Bradley states 'Marsh, never a strong man physically, suffered a breakdown in the latter part of 1910'.

As a result, in February 1911, Marsh went abroad to convalesce and recover. A note in the *Brighton Herald* for 18th March headed 'Illness of D. Earle Marsh' intimated: 'A fortnight ago we announced that Mr D. Earle Marsh had obtained a lengthy leave of absence, and that his place as Engineer of the Brighton Railway Works was temporarily being filled by Mr Billinton. Mr Marsh has gone away for the benefit of his health. He is now in Lausanne, Switzerland, undergoing a course of treatment under the direction of a specialist'. Meanwhile, according to the local *Pike's Guide,* all correspondence was to be directed to 'The Office' at Brighton station. The Brighton & Hove Natural History Society had arranged for a visit of the railway works on 13th March, and found themselves escorted by Basil Field.

The Brighton Board had stipulated that Marsh hand over his office temporarily and be 'granted leave of absence from duties until 1st June next, and that Mr L.B. Billinton, District Locomotive Superintendent at New Cross take general charge of the Locomotive and Carriage work as the locum tenens of the Locomotive Engineer during his absence'. On 31st May the Board granted an extension to Marsh's leave of absence to 30th June, 1911.

The fact is that Marsh was to recover, assume a consultancy and live for another 20 years.

Interim Measures

Meanwhile the locomotive crisis continued. On 1st March the Board had asked for monthly, not quarterly statements of work in progress in the Locomotive Department with numbers of engines under or awaiting repairs. The Chairman had inspected Brighton works with Mr Billinton and had stressed the importance of making engine repairs the paramount consideration to the exclusion, if necessary, of renewal repairs. The Board now spelt this out, authorising Billinton to give his first consideration to repair of engines with the least possible delay, if necessary postponing renewal work by half a year.

On 12th July, 1911 the newly appointed Locomotive Committee, comprising three members of the Board and the acting locomotive engineer, submitted their first report prefaced by the statement, 'The Committee has proceeded on the assumption that the proposals with regard to the retirement of Mr Marsh will be duly completed'. Foremost, it had directed its attention to the present position and organisation of the Locomotive, Carriage and Wagon Department, and its future conduct and management. 'Mr Marsh has been incapacitated from duty by reason of ill health since the beginning of February.' The Committee assumed there would be no way back for Marsh and therefore chose this opportune moment to reorganise this huge elephantine department to more manageable constituents.

Since Marsh's sick leave 'L.B. Billinton has general control except that Mr Panter, Manager of the Carriage and Wagon construction branch has dealt interdependently with matters relating to that branch'. They went on to authorise that,

> . . . until 31st December L.B. Billinton would be in charge of the locomotive branch of the Department with managerial control of construction and repair shops, works and other business, and that the Carriage and Wagon section of the branch be permanently separated and formed into an independent department with A.H. Panter in charge of management and control of works and business at Lancing and Brighton.

Additionally the Board would require monthly statements of (a) electric train miles, (b) engine stock and engine workings, (c) engines stopped for repair, and that quarterly meetings of this new committee would continue.

Marsh, however, was not yet off the agenda. The minutes of 19th July mentioned 'A report of Mr Marsh upon the work of the Locomotive, Carriage and Wagon Department was laid on the table'. Whether this was an opportunity to explain and account for the current situation, especially as regards locomotives, or a 'state of the nation' report for the benefit of his successors, or both, is not stated.

Another item was an application by Mr Marsh for an allowance from the Pension Fund by reason of ill health. It was agreed 'a sum equal to six month's salary be paid to Mr Marsh *as a mark of the Board's appreciation of his service to the Company during his tenure of office as Locomotive and Carriage Engineer*, and a cheque in his favour drawn accordingly'. It was confirmed that the Pension Fund Managing Committee had granted the application by Mr Marsh for an allowance by reason of ill health and that this would continue to run from 1st July at which time Mr Marsh's duties had ceased.

The second report of the Locomotive Committee was presented on 18th October, 1911. A majority of the Board were in favour of approaching Robert Urie of the LSWR, but he saw his future at Eastleigh and requested not to be considered. It gave further consideration to making the interim arrangements permanent. 'Mr Lawson Butzkopfski [sic] Billinton' was now appointed locomotive engineer of the company at a salary of £1,000 pa, upped to £1,500 from 1st January, 1912 with assistance from Mr John Richardson as outdoor locomotive superintendent of the many running sheds and of the locomotives working. The latter's salary was increased to £750 pa. Mr Albert Harry Panter was to be appointed carriage and wagon superintendent at a salary of £750 pa with control of Lancing and Brighton and the work of cleaning carriages was to be supervised by him. A grant of £105 (100 guineas) was to be made to each of the above mentioned gentlemen in consideration of the additional work and responsibility thrown upon them during the present year with effect from 1st December, 1911. All new construction work proposed by either of the Rolling Stock Departments was to be submitted to the Committee in future before being put in hand.

The shake up and consequent promotions also embraced Brighton works. On 20th December, 1911 it was agreed 'that Mr Basil Kingsford Field, now Chief Draughtsman at Brighton be appointed Works Manager of the Locomotive shops at £420 pa, and his assistant Chief Draughtsman, James Martin Jackson to be appointed Chief Draughtsman at £300 pa'. William Thomas Glendenning, the erecting shop foreman was appointed outdoor mechanical inspector at the several locomotive depots at £250 pa.

A Brighton Cover-Up

Comparing the company's minutes with the rumours and aspersions in circulation, suggests that there may well have been a deliberate exercise by Brighton officialdom to kick over the traces. On the face of it, in the context of a century ago, one would have expected nothing less. It was the honourable and gentlemanly thing to do to avoid open scandal detrimental to the company and to allow Marsh to move on without affecting his chances of rebuilding a future career at a time when he was only nudging 50. It is impossible to believe that the Directors were unaware of Marsh's shortcomings, and they seized on his bill of ill health to part company and take the opportunity to reform the ailing Locomotive Department. In doing so they recognised that, among his many mixed achievements some had been outstandingly good and, by way of easing their conscience, voted a handshake as well as retaining him on full pay for several months following his indisposition, and also dipping generously into the company's Pension Fund - in all not a bad 'financial package'.

Chapter Eight

Insight

Basil Kingsford Field

It has been said that in this life those who get the credit for anything seldom are the ones that did the work. When it comes to making an assessment of Marsh's contribution to the Locomotive Department, one needs to take into account a new school of revisionist locomotive historians coming to the fore who feel strongly that the credit for successful motive power design should at least be shared between the engineer and his chief draughtsman and assistants and, in some exceptional circumstances, to attribute the lion's share to the latter. As with Robert Surtees to Harry Wainwright on the SECR, so too tribute needs to be paid to the considerable contribution made by Basil Field which has been largely overlooked.

Late in 1906, Marsh, whose reputation at Doncaster had been described as 'taciturn', recommended to the Board the appointment of B.K. Field to the position of chief draughtsman at Brighton. The obituary in *The Locomotive* for 15th December, 1941 gives a summary of his career. Born in 1866, Field had been educated at Dulwich College, at Heidelberg in Germany and at King's College, London, with technical training at the Crystal Palace School of Engineering and the City and Guilds of London Technical Institute. He served an apprenticeship in the Ashford works of the South Eastern Railway (SER) before entering the drawing office in 1888. In 1897 he became chief locomotive draughtsman there under James Stirling but, with the formation of the South Eastern and Chatham Railways Managing Committee, he had to bow to the seniority of Robert Surtees of the London, Chatham & Dover Railway.

Godfrey Yeomans suggests that, rather than undergo an unspecified period of unemployment when the two companies entered upon their working union on New Year's Day 1899, Field was content to wait his time and meanwhile keep himself in pocket and continue under Surtees until such time as a suitable post came up.

On 25th March, 1902 John H. Adams (son of the LSWR's William) was appointed the North Staffordshire Railway (NSR) locomotive superintendent. He had been a colleague of Field's at Ashford works and renewed his close working relationship by appointing Field to the combined position of chief draughtsman and works manager at Stoke on 1st July. Three months later Field left to begin a brief flirtation with the fledgling motor car industry as works manager of the Motor Manufacturing Company at Coventry in 1903. He was retained by the NSR for a while as locomotive draughtsman. Even in his short time on the NSR he made his mark, for the January 1904 Railway *Magazine* makes reference to Field's patent features, and especially commented on the shapely chimney evolved from the final Stirling SER 4-4-0s which remained the standard NSR feature up to 1923.

At the end of November 1905 a vacancy for the post of chief draughtsman at Brighton came about through the resignation of George Gillies through ill health, 'as a result of the special work and responsibility thrown upon him during the illness of the late Mr Billinton when he was practically the head of the Department'. A Mr Spidy stood in as acting chief draughtsman but, following the reduction of Mr Spidy, the way was open for Marsh to fill the position permanently, choosing a man with an experienced track record.

Appointed as chief locomotive draughtsman at Brighton on 19th December, 1906 to start his new post with effect from 1st January, 1907, at £250 pa raised to £300 from 1st July, Field immediately stamped his personality on all the Brighton's locomotives. He quickly got to grips with design of the 'I3' class, as already described in some detail, and then moved on to the 'H2' Atlantics. He was responsible for the modified Ramsbottom safety valves housed in a very elegantly curved iron casting, the plump closed top Marsh dome, and the massive cast-iron chimney. The 4-6-2T *Abergavenny of* 1910 must have been one of the most handsome ever built. Marsh is recorded as having been particularly interested in this locomotive on his weekly visits to the works. Hamilton Ellis describes Field as 'unclubbable and unapproachable, engineer and artist, for certainly it was he who moved his chief into the superheating realm and thereby initiated a little revolution in the motive power of British express passenger traffic. For all his austerity, Field was a diplomat'.

In the restructuring that followed Marsh's departure, he was promoted to locomotive works manager, on 20th December, 1911 at £420 pa under Lawson Billinton and continued through to February 1924, taking early retirement from the Southern Railway as a result of Maunsell's reorganisation of the CME's Department. A Mr Buckle, a colleague at Brighton, who wrote his obituary in *The Locomotive Magazine* for 15th December, 1941 stated: 'After retirement Mr Field devoted most of his leisure time to model engineering. His sense of humour and fund of anecdote endeared him to a large circle of friends'. Basil Field died at Brighton on 15th November, 1941.

A portrait of Basil Kingsford Field at his very tidy desk at Brighton works where he was promoted from chief draughtsman to works manager starting on New Year's Day 1912, the date the promotion took effect, at a salary of £420 pa.

Marsh's Later Life

Marsh did not immediately leave the arena for on 16th December, 1911 Mr and Mrs D.E. Marsh were reported as attending the Mayor's Ball in Brighton. Marsh had married somewhat late in life. On 15th November, 1906 he was wedded to Gladys Mary Lyttelton Annesley in St Patrick's Church, Hove. The Annesley family lived at nearby 36 Adelaide Crescent. The wedding was well attended by the Marsh clan and three of the witnesses to the signing belonged specifically to the Earle Marsh branch. Gladys married at 23 while Douglas is recorded as of 'full age' though only in fact 44.

Jack Annesley Earle Marsh, 'a honeymoon babe', was born to them in the late summer of 1907 and two years later a daughter, Patricia Catherine. Jack was only six years old when Marsh vacated the official accommodation provided by the railway company. The records show that Lawson Billinton did not move in, his official address being given as 'Central Station, Queen's Road, Brighton'. In fact the latter was living in a flat overlooking the seafront at Brighton and, on becoming CME, the LB&SCR placed at his disposal another company house in Silverdale Avenue as Marsh was still ensconced at No.3 Chichester Terrace at the time. The latter was presumably disposed of by the railway company in 1913 as an unknown name then appears in *Pike's Directory for Brighton and Hove*. The house no longer stands.

Soon after leaving the company, Marsh had found new employment, joining the Rio Tinto mining company as a consulting engineer, and acted in this capacity until 1932. During these years he commuted up to the capital with spasmodic visits to the company's mines in southern Spain.

In 1913 he purchased the freehold of No. 47 The Drive, Hove. It may be asked how Marsh was able to purchase such a substantial property amongst the exclusive villas of Hove. It must have cost a pretty penny. This could have been purchased using most of the £750 'handshake' granted by the company following his resignation. On the other hand his wife was part Lyttelton, and Lord Lyttelton was the paterfamilias of a well endowed landed family, while the Annesleys were an Irish land-owning family. Marsh had certainly married into wealth. Moreover by this time Marsh was already drawing an income from the Rio Tinto, his new employers.

The freehold house at 47 The Drive provided the occasion for a new will revoking former testamentary dispositions, being witnessed on 10th January, 1916, in which he appointed his step-brother, Captain Augustus Charles Earle Marsh of the Royal Field Artillery and Royal Flying Corps as his executor. He was to receive a legacy of £500 and Marsh's brother Herbert Charles £100. He left the main estate to his wife and gave instructions to his trustees for investments to be made in stocks and funds on his wife's behalf.

A study of this will in relation to the four codicils that followed helps to fill in some of the details of the sparsely recorded later period of his life. In the codicil of 14th October, 1926 he revoked the appointment of his step-brother and appointed instead Lieutenant General Gerard Prideaux Tharn and Maurice Ferrier, a Geneva banker, with a bequest of £200 each for carrying out their duties. The second codicil was necessary because in 1927 Marsh had moved

Marriage certificate of Douglas Earle Marsh dated 15th November, 1906.
Courtesy General Register Office

This picture was found amongst the Marsh Collection lodged with the Firefly Trust, and is believed to be of Mrs Marsh with Jack and his sister seated on the right while the young lady on the left is presumed to be the governess. The unknown location could well be one of the country mansions belonging to Mrs Marsh's well connected family.   *The Firefly Trust*

with his family from Hove to Batheaston House in Somerset, a few miles outside Bath.

In the third codicil, dated 2nd October, 1930, Marsh revoked the £5,000 legacy to his wife in favour of an absolute share and life interest in his residuary estate. He also cut down the legacy of his step-brother to a mere £100, and gave to each of his children a legacy of £500. Also of interest here is the fact that one of the witnesses to the codicil was a Fred Higley, butler at Batheaston House, indicating the affluence of the Marsh household at that period. However, this relative prosperity was not to last for, by the final codicil dated 2nd May, 1932, right in the middle of the inter-war economic depression, 'in view of the heavy depreciation of my investments', Marsh cut back the £200 bequests to his executors to just £50. One of the witnesses was Frederick Morgan, manservant of his who hailed from nearby Trowbridge.

Marsh died on 25th May, 1933, Ascension Day, and was interred in the churchyard at Batheaston Parish Church. Probate was granted on 19th July that year declaring the gross value of the estate and effects was £30,615 17s. 4d., which, in money terms of that period, stood up well in comparison with the lesser gentry. But all was not plain sailing for the will was disputed, leading to an awful family row which is still remembered in the locality. Apparently a claimant, surely not Marsh's step-brother, appeared giving the impression that he was down and out - shades again of the Robert Leaman case - who might only have learned at this stage of his being brushed aside as an executor with a much reduced legacy.

Obituaries appeared in the *Railway Gazette* (page 94) of 2nd June, 1933 and in the *Proceedings of the Institute of Civil Engineers* (page 475) the following year. The former spoke of his producing in five years,

> . . . designs which left a notable mark upon the history of locomotives of this country. To him the adaptation of the tank engine for express passenger working with 6 ft 7 in. and even 6 ft 9 in. wheels is due, and he was also an advocate and firm supporter of the hot water feed system and of superheating in its infancy in Britain. Many of his locomotives, including 4-4-2 and 4-6-2 tank and 4-4-2 tender engines are still employed on the SR's fast and often heavy expresses.

However, people who knew him in Bath described him as 'not a person one could know, doubtless a brilliant engineer, but brusque and unpredictable outside his field'.

When his wife died after a long widowhood, aged 89, the house, looking very run down in the end, had to be sold to divide the estate between the children. In the funeral register she is described as an 'Earle Marsh'. There is an unusual annotation in the grave records at Batheaston Parish Church stating that she 'drove a Jaguar sports car with a speed governed to 30 mph'.

Jack Marsh moved into humbler quarters inside Bath. His railway career was not pursued and he went into collecting vintage cars, a trait doubtless gleaned from his father's keen motoring interests. It must have been he who provided his aged mother with the above castrated Jaguar. Though his wife Betty was well liked by the ladies of the town, locals maintained Jack never fitted into the civic life of Bath. He suffered from deteriorating eyesight and spent most daytimes socialising in the pub in the years preceding his recent death.

47, The Drive, Hove, where Marsh and his family lived from 1914 to 1927. It is definitely not the house shown in the previous picture.

An Appraisal

Charles Fryer in his book *The Locomotives of D. Earle Marsh* rates Marsh 'in the second eleven of locomotive engineers', fair comment provided one takes into account the balance of his successes and failures. Some have attributed his steady rise up the ladder of promotion to personal connections, asking whether he had influence in high places as he did not seem to be an outstanding designer or manager. Yet he managed to get three good positions during his life, namely assistant locomotive works manager at Swindon, chief assistant mechanical engineer and manager of the Great Northern's Doncaster works, and No. 1 at Brighton. To be fair to the man, he must have convinced the interviewing boards of a considerable degree of ability in order to pip his rivals.

As to locomotive design, it is not easy to accord proportionate credit between the contributions made by the chief engineer and the team under his chief draughtsman. Certainly Marsh was an ideas man, witness his interest in differing up and coming forms of motive traction, together with his penchant for experimentation with a view to improving performance. Yet in the nitty-gritty of detail Basil Field deserves more credit than he is usually given. The chief locomotive engineer needs to be the man of vision with an ability to inspire and use his drawing office team to render the project a success. Marsh certainly had an inventive mind as he viewed the needs of the Brighton Locomotive Department, and all inventors are generally permitted to have failures as part of the price leading up to some stunning success. The Great Central's J.G. Robinson has been described as one of the successful designers of the 'British hit-and-miss' school of locomotive engineers, and Earle Marsh would certainly qualify to belong to that category.

Ben Webb in his brief analysis of Marsh writes: 'Though his regime as Brighton locomotive chief was brief, it was drastic, producing a similar effect to that caused by Cromwell's Ironsides when they campaigned against worldly pleasure and clothed England with its first government ordained garbs of austerity'. True, the financially overstretched Brighton Board were in a penny-pinching mood, and disappearance of the lavish and ornate Stroudley livery and the majority of names was there for all to see. However, one can question whether this 'atmosphere of severity' in the context of the extravagant and exciting Edwardian era impressed itself on the travelling public as opposed to railway enthusiasts of the day.

Where Marsh fell short was in his relations with his men. He arrived at Brighton like a new injudicious headmaster, intent on implementing fresh ideas, having failed to realise the good qualities in so much of the equipment and workforce responsible for the good functioning of the company borne out of years of experience. From 'Day One' he found himself continually on the defensive, battling against a workforce that proved to be one of the most diehard and conservative in the whole country. On many occasions they led Marsh a dance as they dug in their heels against change and modernisation. The ill will against a 'furrin' Doncaster man was there from the start and Marsh knew it and had to face it at a time when the fledgling trade unions were flexing their muscles. Such improvements in the works and among the footplate men were won at some cost against the dogged and obdurate resistance of the men and the unions behind them.

To be fair to Marsh, he had his hands tied with regard to what he could offer, the company during the later period of his office finding itself in dire financial stringency and leaving him with no flexibility whatever to meet the demands of the men. However, he could have shown a greater degree of concern for their welfare, as was so openly apparent in the regime of his successor. Positions remained polarised between management and worker with constant deadlock and threats from both sides. He had to toil against whispering campaigns and subtle innuendo from the men under him and, though there was little truth in most of them, they left their marks in sustained damage to his reputation.

Another area in which he found himself in a no-win situation was that of economy. Charles Fryer, referring to the astonishing low coal and water consumption rates of the 'I3' tanks, states: 'As an economist Marsh served his Company well'. Possibly in a few cases, as here and over liveries, substantial savings were effected, but hardly anywhere else, for there was huge pressure from the top to achieve far lower costings. However, when discussing the fiasco, Fryer's verdict was that 'a potentially good engine had been spoiled in order to produce economies which turned out not to be achievable'. Marsh in seeking to achieve economies made a number of false ones which only exacerbated the motive power situation.

As to Marsh's character, one can sense a degree of arrogance, impatience, obduracy and testiness which did not endear him to the workforce. No one has previously drawn up a portrait of the man, and all we are left with to make some kind of an assessment is the first-hand record of his dealings with the union deputations. There his character and personality are laid bare for future historians to make their judgements.

But when it comes to his moral character we are left groping. There was obviously a mercenary streak in his personality, a common one in any day or age. Was Marsh was no different from the hotel guest who goes off with the soap or the cutlery, except on an altogether larger scale? Many jobs have perks, and there is a thinly defined line where perks end and thieving begins. Unfortunately the few misdemeanours that actually took place were blown out of all proportion by the sheer weight of gossip, prattle and rumour as media and workforce homed in on Marsh's patent unpopularity and brittle character. Finance, or rather the lack of it, did seem to be a weak point in his armour. All was lost at one fell throw, although one suspects it was the culmination of a succession of alleged underhand dealings.

Marsh retired to a consultancy post and continued to live in some style on his reasonable pension. Worst of all he had to live with his tragic past, a disgraced and fallen man in his own eyes who had missed out on unblemished success. One would perhaps be going too far to suggest he was made a scapegoat for the ills of the company, though it has to be conceded that the traumas of the Locomotive Department, which was under his control, were to a degree of his making. He had been placed in a position of responsibility and he was therefore held to account. His tracks were covered by the sterling efforts of his Brighton employers to conceal his indiscretions, for their good as well as his. And for that reason, with a distinct lack of information surviving, we shall unfortunately never know the full story. Perhaps, when all that can be said is done, the best outcome is to let matters lie as they are.

Bibliography and Sources

Books
C.J. Binnie - *The Brighton Terriers* (Ravensbourne 1969)
G. Bixley *et al* - *An Illustrated History of Southern Wagons Vol. 2 - LB&SCR and minor Companies* (OPC 1985)
D.L. Bradley - *Locomotives of the LB&SCR Vols 1, 2 and 3* (RCTS 1969-74)
Anthony Bulleid - *Master Builders of Steam* (Ian Allan 1963)
F. Burtt - *The Locomotives of the London, Brighton and South Coast Railway 1839-1903* (LPC 1903)
H.J. Campbell Cornwall - *William Stroudley - Craftsman of Steam* (David & Charles 1968)
B.K. Casper - *Rail Centres - Brighton* (Ian Allan 1981)
C. Hamilton Ellis - The *London, Brighton and South Coast Railway* (Ian Allan 1960)
Charles Fryer - *The Locomotives of D. Earle Marsh* (Ebor Press 1994)
David Gould - *Bogie Carriages of the London, Brighton and South Coast Railway* (Oakwood Press 1995)
Roger Griffiths - *Southern Sheds in Camera* (OPC 1989)
Handel Kardas - *Portrait of the Terriers* (Ian Allan 1999)
R.A.S. Hennessey - *Atlantic* (Tempus 2002)
J.E. Kite - *Vintage Steam* (1969)
J.N. Maskelyne - *Locomotives I have known* (Argus 1959)
J.N. Maskelyne - *The Locomotives of the London, Brighton and South Coast Railway 1903-1923* (LPC 1928)
P.J. Newberry - *Carriage Stock of the LB&SCR* (Oakwood 1976)
A.C. Perryman - *When Steam was King at Brighton* (Rochester Press 1982)
F. Rich - *Yesterday Once More* (PWA 1996)
Peter Q. Treloar - *The Earle Marsh Album* (Firefly Trust 1985)
Ben Webb - *Locomotive Engineers of the Southern Railway* (Ian Allan 1946)
G.A. Yeomans - *A Brighton Locomotive Chronology Parts 1-3* (Privately Published 2002)

Documents (At the National Archives)
Rail 414 83 *Brighton Board of Directors Meeting*
Rail 414 164 *Finance Committee on 'Stores Matters'*
Rail 414 184 *Locomotive and Construction Committee*
Rail 414 260/1 *Extracts from Minutes and Board Orders*
Rail 414 536 *Use of Automobiles on Railway* - Philip Dawson
Rail 414 641 *Locomotive and Carriage Department Expenditure*
Rail 414 758 *Staff Meetings with the Locomotive Engineer*
The Probate Department, Holborn
General Register Office, Southport

Journals, Magazines and Newspapers
Dr Ian C. Allen - Some LB&SC Reminiscences - *Southern Notebook* No. 93 (SRG 1987)
Dr Ian C. Allen - SR Class 'D1x' 0-4-2T B216 and other matters - *Southern Notebook* No. 101 (SRG 1989)
L.E. Brailsford - The Brailsford Diaries - *The Brighton Circular* - Vols 27-29 (2001-3)
W.E. Briggs - Brighton Works 1902-1939 - *Southern Railway Magazine* (1940)
Derek Cross - The Larger Brighton Locomotives - *Locomotives Illustrated* No. 37 (Ian Allan 1984)
Marcus Gaywood - Disappointing Locomotives - *Southern Notebook* No. 85 (SRG 1985)
R.H.N. Hardy - The Brighton Atlantics - *Steam World* - Issue No. 173 (Emap 2001)
A.C. Perryman - Speaking up for the Brighton Railway History - *Trains Illustrated* No. 54 (Ian Allan 1985)
Brighton Gazette
Brighton Herald
Sussex Daily News
Pikes Directory of Brighton and Hove
Proceedings of the Institute of Civil Engineers (1934)
Railway Gazette D.E. Marsh Obituary - 2nd June, 1933
The Locomotive D.E. Marsh Obituary - 15th June, 1933
The Locomotive B.K. Field Obituary - 15th December, 1941

Index